DOGTIPS from DOGTOWN

A RELATIONSHIP MANUAL
for You *and* Your Dog

Best Friends Animal Society Trainers
with Michael S. Sweeney

NATIONAL GEOGRAPHIC

Washington, D.C.

Published by the National Geographic Society
1145 17th Street N.W., Washington, D.C. 20036

Library of Congress Cataloging-in-Publication Data

Dog tips from dogtown : a relationship manual for you and your dog /
Best Friends Animal Society trainers with Michael S. Sweeney.
   p. cm.
Includes bibliographical references and index.
ISBN 978-1-4262-0648-1 (hardcover)
1. Dogs--Training. 2. Human-animal relationships. I. Sweeney,
Michael S. II. Best Friends Animal Society.
SF431.D64 2010
636.7--dc22
                                          2010025530

The National Geographic Society is one of the world's largest nonprofit scientific and educational organizations. Founded in 1888 to "increase and diffuse geographic knowledge," the Society works to inspire people
to care about the planet. National Geographic reflects the world through its magazines, television programs, films, music and radio, books, DVDs, maps, exhibitions, live events, school publishing programs,
interactive media and merchandise. *National Geographic* magazine, the Society's official journal, published
in English and 32 local—language editions, is read by more than 35 million people each month. The
National Geographic Channel reaches 320 million households in 34 languages in 166 countries. National
Geographic Digital Media receives more than 13 million visitors a month. National Geographic has funded
more than 9,200 scientific research, conservation and exploration projects and supports an education program promoting geography literacy. For more information, visit nationalgeographic.com.

For more information, please call 1-800-NGS LINE
(647-5463) or write to the following address:

National Geographic Society
1145 17th Street N.W.
Washington, D.C. 20036-4688 U.S.A.

For information about special discounts for bulk purchases,
please contact National Geographic Books Special Sales: ngspecsales@ngs.org

For rights or permissions inquiries, please contact National Geographic Books
Subsidiary Rights: ngbookrights@ngs.org

Interior design: Linda Makarov and Cameron Zotter

Printed in the U.S.A.

10/QGF/1

Contents

Foreword

I am an animal lover . . . from the magnificent wildlife of my native South Africa to the dogs and cats that have been my household companions over the years. They enrich my life and make me happy. Like most people who have pets, I love to be able to see them run around and play, enjoying the protected life that I am able to provide for them.

Part of giving my pets a good life includes being able to provide training, especially when there is a serious behavior issue, they have trouble learning the rules of the house, or they have to learn how to get along with the other four-footed family members. I often turn to Best Friends for help and guidance, so I'm really pleased that this book of dog-training tips from Best Friends Dogtown is now available to everyone.

Best Friends shares my love and respect for the animals, and I know you will find their gentle, patient approach to training helpful in building a loving relationship with your dog. And please, be sure to adopt your next pet from a local shelter or rescue organization.

—Charlize Theron
Actress and Best Friends Member

Introduction

The relationship between humans and dogs is nothing new. To date, the best evidence suggests that we share a relationship going back at least 14,000 years. No one knows how it all started—whether we chose human-tolerant wolves to assist us with hunting and protection or if those wolves actually decided to live with us for food and the other perks humanity provided. However the relationship developed, we are now stuck with each other. The dogs that we live with today are hardwired by millennia of purposeful breeding for a relationship with people, and who's to say that humanity's wiring to desire a relationship with dog has not been affected by our partnership with these remarkable creatures. Being guided by our shared instincts and common history brings us together into the most successful, unique interspecies relationship on the planet. And our relationships can only get better by further adapting how we relate to dogs in a way that respects their intelligence, their individuality, and their desire for our companionship.

Dogtown is one of the primary animal care areas at Best Friends Animal Sanctuary, the home of Best Friends Animal Society. As the name implies, Best Friends believes that the animals in our care and in our home are our friends. They are not captives, slaves, or enemies that need to be forced into compliance. Neither are they animated toys that only need to be programmed. They are intelligent beings with a full range of interests, emotions, needs, and sometimes an unknown personal history. In short—they have lives of their own. Dog training at Best Friends, or should I say "dog education," begins with a respect for the long history that we share and the understanding that every dog is an individual, just like you and me. Consider this: Teaching a happy, well-nurtured puppy is very different from teaching a dog that has been abused which is different from teaching a dog that has learned to manage his life and environment in ways that are just not appropriate for hanging out with or living with people. Living with each of these dogs and giving him the best life possible requires a different strategy for each one. You'll need to discard any previous assumptions and get to know the dog as an individual in order to build a strong, trust-based relationship between the two of you.

At Dogtown, the philosophy and ethics of Best Friends Animal Society is apparent in the methodology that our amazing staff applies to teaching the dogs in our care. We show dogs how to succeed in the lives that are awaiting them when they leave the sanctuary and are adopted into loving new homes through an approach called Relationship-Based Training. As the name implies, it's not about coercion or force, it's about building a friendship, one that works for both parties involved. Just like any other relationship it involves an exchange of information and a consistent "language" that allows mutual comfort and trust to grow.

You *want* a successful relationship with your dog, but your dog *needs* a successful relationship with you. The guidelines, insights, and tips contained in this book have been proven over years of working with dogs of all ages and with almost every imaginable prior experience including the trauma of Hurricane Katrina, the abuses of dogfighting rings, the shock of war, or the simple dislocation resulting from economic hardship. *Dog Tips from Dogtown* will help you and your dog to get the most out of your relationship and to become truly, best friends.

—Francis Battista
Co-founder, Best Friends Animal Society

When thinking about adopting, consider how different dogs can be from each other, like this group of diverse dogs hanging out with trainer Whitney Jones.

Know
Yourself

Sometimes you adopt a dog. Sometimes a dog seems to adopt you. Sometimes you both just know: It's mutual, an interspecies love at first sight.

In any case, your choice to share your life with a dog will bring dramatic changes, both emotional and practical. You will take on the greatest responsibility you can imagine, short of caring for another human being. You will experience higher highs and lower lows. You may learn the true meaning of unconditional love.

For these reasons, adopting a dog should not be done lightly.

Take the love affair between a long-haired mutt named Dundee Boy and a couple—Yvette and Francisco—from just outside Chicago. They had supported animal rescue operations before becoming members of Best Friends Animal Society, the nation's largest sanctuary for homeless animals. In May 2006, Yvette and Francisco decided to take a service vacation to the society's 3,700-acre sanctuary in the majestic red rock country of Kanab, Utah. Before they left, the couple made a vow not to adopt any animals. Their condominium just didn't have room for a family expansion.

But life has a habit of surprising you when you think you're most prepared.

Best Friends encourages volunteers to have sleepovers with dogs awaiting adoption. Visitors can stay overnight with a dog in one of the many cabins and cottages on the Best Friends sanctuary grounds, or at one of the hotels in nearby Kanab that accommodates pets. The sleepover provides an opportunity for dogs to learn socialization skills and enjoy human companionship. For the volunteers, a sleepover provides relaxation and fun with a needy dog. Many potential adopters use the time as a "test-drive" to see the dog in a homelike environment away from a shelter. Yvette and Francisco planned to take a dog for a sleepover, always reminding themselves they had no plans to adopt.

Then they met Dundee Boy. He had come to Dogtown, Best Friends' home for cast-off canines, from the San Francisco Society for the Prevention of Cruelty to Animals. He had guarding issues, reacting with too much aggression around food, and wasn't a candidate for a quick adoption. For most of his life, the big black, brown, and white long-haired dog with expressive eyes and a half curl to his lip had been waiting to find what Best Friends calls a "forever home." When Yvette and Francisco saw him, he had just been taken off the "no sleepovers" list. Dundee Boy's behavior had improved enough to earn him approval to go on sleepovers with adults, and the couple chose to spend an evening with him. A caregiver counseled the couple to watch for Dundee Boy's food aggression, but added that the dog was one of Best Friends' "neediest cases."

The couple took Dundee Boy on hikes in the dry canyons and sand dunes of southern Utah. They fed him treats and combed his wild hair. He responded with unbridled affection. When it came time to go back to Chicago, they left with heavy hearts. They missed Dundee Boy.

Yvette and Francisco knew they would have to forsake their oath and adopt Dundee Boy. But how? Their condominium banned dogs of more than 40 pounds, and Dundee Boy packed considerably more heft. The staff at Best Friends joked that Yvette and Francisco ought to take the dog home and plead ignorance of the rule, or say they thought it applied to dogs of 40 *kilograms* instead of pounds. However, Yvette served on the condo's governing board, so that wouldn't work.

In reality, Best Friends caregivers would never send a dog to a place where the rules would make him an outlaw. Their joking merely aimed to relieve the tension of the couple's dilemma: They couldn't live with Dundee Boy, and they couldn't live without him. The situation called for a creative decision. So Yvette and Francisco made a bold move. They left their condo and moved into a spacious house. Then they adopted Dundee Boy and brought him home.

"And Dundee Boy is still there, in that home, and doing great," says Tamara Dormer, a certified dog trainer at Best Friends. "A lot of potential owners would give up, but they are totally committed to him. They adore him."

Many people who come to Dogtown love dogs and have made a choice to adopt those whom others have deemed unadoptable. Dogtown works hard to rehabilitate dogs, restoring their health, assessing and working on any behavioral challenges, and engaging their minds through play and exercise. Dundee Boy's experience shows how, even when a potential family falls in love with a dog, common sense and reason must be a part of bringing that dog into your life: For Francisco and Yvette, their self-evaluation led to a need for a new home. Going through the proper steps, with careful consideration of yourself, your home, your family, and the dog you might want to adopt, raises the probability of successful adoption.

Getting the right dog ought to start with you making a candid self-assessment. You should examine your lifestyle, your income, and your home. You should assess why you want a dog and what you are willing to invest into the relationship. Like users of a dating service, you also need to check out your potential partners. What are you looking for in a dog? How might dogs of different ages, sizes, and energy levels fit the profiles you have constructed? Finally, are you really ready to make a lifelong commitment?

Lessons From Dog University

Best Friends Animal Society is a great place to begin understanding dogs and their relationships with people. Since its founding in the early 1980s, Best Friends has devoted itself to the idea that kindness to animals creates a better world. At Best Friends, as many as 1,700 animals, including several hundred dogs, receive care and attention at a time. Animals arrive at Best Friends from many different places and circumstances, including shelters and rescue groups, often just days before they may have been scheduled to be put to death. Typically, they have special behavioral or physical needs that have overwhelmed their previous caregivers or defied solutions. Best Friends offers a last chance at redemption. Best Friends does not euthanize any animal except to relieve pain and illness. It promotes adoption as a key tool to end euthanasia of unwanted pets, which claims approximately four million to five million pets a year in America.

When animals come to Best Friends, staff members and volunteers work with them to get them ready for adoption. Veterinarians treat any wounds and diseases; caregivers and volunteers provide food, water, exercise, and a safe, clean place to live; and trainers encourage the healthy habits of well-socialized animals and try to resolve any behavioral problems that might interfere with a successful adoption. All provide the love and understanding that every dog needs. With patience and love, dogs labeled elsewhere—sometimes incorrectly—as incorrigibly shy, violent, or vicious work toward becoming good citizens of Dogtown and on their way to adoption. Aggressive animals learn tolerance. Undersocialized animals, such as those raised in puppy mills, gain confidence. Dogs trained to kill other dogs in the ring for sport can improve their social skills and learn to tolerate other dogs. Even many of the dogs seized from NFL quarterback Michael Vick's dogfighting ring in Virginia have rebounded and are living well-adjusted lives at Best Friends and in their new adoptive homes. Any dogs unable to be adopted are able to live out the remainder of their lives in a nurturing environment—perhaps the first they have ever known.

Through its work at the Utah sanctuary and a nationwide network of friends and supporters, Best Friends rehabilitates thousands of dogs every year. The staff and volunteers learn the most positive, effective dog-training techniques and then apply them to their charges. This combination of academic smarts and practical experience, applied day after day to hundreds of dogs, makes Best Friends a sort of university of all things dog-related. In choosing, evaluating, and training dogs, this team of experts knows what makes an adoption work well. It starts with knowing yourself.

Knowing What You Want

Ask yourself some probing questions before you adopt a dog. What are you looking for? A couch companion? An active playmate? A pet for your family?

Best Friends requires potential adopters to complete a dog application questionnaire (available on its website as well as at the facility) so they'll think deeply about such issues. It asks for everything from makeup of the household to the applicant's history of having pets to something as fine-tuned as whether the applicant has a swimming pool. Adoptions don't necessarily hinge on the answers. The application is only a starting point. A follow-up interview provides an opportunity to elaborate. The questions in both the questionnaire and interview cover three main topics: the applicant, the dog, and things that might enhance or harm their relationship.

The most common reason for dog adoption is to gain a new member of the family. You may feel as if there's a missing piece in the puzzle of your life, a hole that you think only a dog can fill. That's an excellent reason to adopt, as long as you're willing to make a lifetime commitment to your pet and not return her when some other puzzle piece comes along that looks even better.

"I think it's wrong to say that emotional attachment is a poor reason to adopt a pet," Best Friends certified dog trainer Whitney Jones says. "That's why I get my dogs. But don't get a dog just so the kids can have a playmate or you can have a jogging partner. You should be emotionally involved as well. The agenda you have in mind may not work out. You may get someone else who jogs with you, and there goes your jogging partner." Or your children may lose interest and neglect the family dog. Or you may not stick to your jogging goals, New Year's resolutions being so easily broken. You should consider whether you can commit to a lifelong relationship regardless of how your life changes.

It is not a good idea to adopt a dog as a trial run for having a baby. Dogs and children have different needs and different bonds with adults. However, a dog's behavior strikes many of the same emotional and psychological chords as parenthood. A dog is inquisitive, playful, needy, dependent, and loving. He requires structure and stimulation. From puppyhood to old age, his actions may seem to mirror those of a permanently four-year-old human, alternating between some behavior that tests the limits of adult patience and other behavior that radiates pure love.

To adopt a dog, you must have a modicum of patience and a temper that's under control. Dogs make mistakes. Responding to a mess on the carpet or a chewed-up book demands a measured response and some calm analysis of why the problem occurred. Getting angry and yelling only make the problem worse in the long run by sowing the seeds of distrust and fear in the relationship. However, it's possible to learn greater patience as you work with your dog. Like a muscle, patience grows stronger when exercised.

Adopting a dog can change a person. "I have seen people change their personality completely, or things they may love, just because of their dog," Tamara says. "I see people who started out just wanting a dog. And when I go to visit them, their whole life has changed. Now they're friends with people at the dog park. They may never have gone hiking; now they're doing that so their dogs can get exercise." When Tamara adopted her own dog, Buck, a yellow Lab, it completely changed her life. She had been living a somewhat circumscribed life in a North Carolina city. Buck got her outdoors more, meeting people, enjoying training, and eventually into her career as a dog trainer.

But change doesn't always happen. It's good for adopters to consider their personalities and their lifestyles to help them pick the right dog. If they have plenty of free time and enjoy exercising in the fresh air, they might choose a dog that needs lots of stimulation. Those with a quieter lifestyle, or who have few free hours at home, would do better with a dog that doesn't require so much activity. To assess the time you can devote to a dog, chart your activities each day, marking the time you spend on work, chores, study, and so on. If you have little free time, you may be doing a dog a favor by choosing *not* to adopt.

If you've recently lost a pet and are searching for a new one, it's best not to try to replace the companion you've lost. Sometimes, the staff at Best Friends will get a special request for a dog just like one who has recently passed away. "We don't say no," Tamara says, "but we stay alert if they say something like, 'This looks exactly like my dog I just lost.' That dog will not be just like the one you lost. He most likely will have a completely different personality." Every dog is an individual, even in the same breed, and looking for an old pet in a new dog can lead to great disappointment on both sides of the relationship.

Who Else Is Around the House?

Assess your family, too. When a household consists of two people, both should endorse the adoption without reservation. Both will need to be involved in training the dog for her to learn to behave properly in a variety of places and for more than one person. Both also should commit to feeding, grooming, and cleaning up the messes. Otherwise, one partner often will end up resenting the dog or the other partner— or both.

If you have children, their maturity and lifestyle may be important. Some dogs aren't good with young children, and some children are just too young to take on responsibility for another life. If children aren't emotionally and mentally prepared for a dog, they can't be counted on to take care of a dog's needs, and caregiving will fall on one or both of the parents.

All family members need to be on board with the decision to adopt a dog and understand their part in caring for a new pet. Consider the age and maturity of each of your children. Experts at

Best Friends can recall five-year-olds who were devoted to caring for their dogs, whereas others—teens (and even some adults)—weren't quite ready for the responsibility yet. You should also consider the schedules of your older children. Are their schedules jam-packed with activities and homework? Will they have time to devote to a new dog? Discuss the adoption with your kids so that everyone knows what's expected of them before the adoption process begins.

Dogs and Kids
Not all dogs are good with kids. Large dogs may be big enough to overwhelm small children with their enthusiasm. Small dogs may look cute but don't always like being smothered by a pint-size embrace. Dogs may see humans as large, threatening figures and disapprove of being picked up or manhandled. If the human is a child, reaching to lift a small dog or bending over to hug a larger dog may put animal and child face to face, a dangerous situation if the dog feels she has to bite to escape.

Still, many dogs form the tightest of bonds with children. Kids often devote more attention and energy to a family dog than do grown-ups, who may have more demands on their time. If you've found a prospective adoptee who has been recommended for placement in a home with children, consider having the dog sleep at your home overnight or fostering him for a while, so you can see how he and your children interact. Keep an eye on the dog whenever he's around your children. And watch your children, too. You'll not only want to monitor dog-and-child interactions to ensure safety, but also to see whether your kids tire of the dog or balk at helping do the daily tasks of taking care of him properly.

But remember that sometimes the best laid plans can go awry: Children may prove unreliable or may be unable to fulfill your care-giving expectations. "A common reason that pets are given up is that the kids lost interest," Whitney says. "Parents have to be prepared for that." It is ultimately the parents' responsibility to be the dog's primary caregivers. Think long and hard about this possibility: It's not fair to a dog or a child to adopt a pet and then return him if the child loses interest. It may communicate to the child that love has conditions and that animals are no different than toys. It doesn't do the dog any good either.

An adopter should also consider how the new dog might fit in with other pets. Some dogs act aggressively toward other animals. Such behavior can be shaped toward a more congenial relationship, but it may never disappear completely.

Potential troubles may be spotted right away; however, sometimes problems don't appear during a sleepover, shelter visit, or an outing. They may crop up at a later time in the relationship when the dog is more comfortable. Prior to finalizing the adoption, fostering a dog (when possible) may provide the best opportunity to see her true personality before taking the final step of adoption. If a formerly feline-friendly dog can't help chasing your cat once she's made the transition to your house, it may be better to discover this problem during a trial run, while you can still decide whether you would be willing to put in the hours to make your pets comfortable with each other, or, if not, to find some way to separate them.

Think Ahead

Consider the future. What if your dogs live many years after your children grow up and leave an empty nest, putting empty nesters in charge of all pet care? If you are single, what will you do if your future spouse has a cat or a dog that your dog doesn't like? You may live in the country and have a 100-acre lot for your border collie to patrol, but what will happen if you get transferred to a city job?

College students may fail to think about the long term when they consider adoption. Young people who leave home and enter the high-stress college environment may adopt a dog for companionship and emotional comfort. Trouble is, when the academic year ends, they may not be able to take the dog home or to a job site.

Change is always uncertain, but you should be honest with yourself about how your pet will fit into any new developments in your life. Try to anticipate solutions that will help keep your dog in the family rather than surrendering him to a shelter. If the only solution you can foresee is to give up the animal, then it's not the best time for you to adopt.

Money and Resources

You'll spend more on a dog than you might think. For an average, medium-size dog, yearly care averages $870 to $1,300, and that covers food, vaccinations, grooming, toys and treats, and optional health insurance. Initial costs also will include a license, collar, and leash, and possibly a crate for housetraining, all of which could add an additional $150 to $200, depending on the size of the dog. These expenses don't include bills for emergency medical care or for adoption fees.

Best Friends requires that all pets already living in a home be spayed or neutered, and current on vaccinations before it will approve an adoption. All dogs at Best Friends are spayed or neutered after their arrival at the sanctuary. Different adoptive groups may have different requirements. Spay and neuter operations are also often required for other rescue and shelter adoptions; the procedure

A Budget for Your Best Friend

Before beginning to adopt, keep in mind the regular costs of ownership. On average, the first year (which includes start-up costs and regular care) can total between $1,300 to $2,100. On average, a medium-size dog can live until age 14, which means you could be looking at roughly $13,000 over the course of a dog's life. Here's a line-by-line breakout:

Start-Up Costs: $500 to $890 Total

- Adoption Fee: $75 to $150 (varies with dog and shelter; fees may include spay/neuter and other medical expenses)
- Spay/Neuter Fee: $190 to $400
- Other Initial Medical Expenses: $70
- Collar/Leash: $25 to $35
- Crate: $35 to $125
- Training Classes: $110 (varies with trainer and class level)

Yearly Costs: $870 to $1,300 Total

- Food: $120 to $235 (premium dry kibble; cost varies depending on size of dog)
- Toys and Treats: $40 to $140
- License: $15 (varies with community)
- Recurring Medical: $210 to $500 (vaccinations, preventative medications, and so on)
- Health Insurance (optional): $225 (varies with policy)
- Grooming: $265 to $408 (costs vary with size of dog and length of hair)

Sources: Best Friends Animal Society; American Society for the Prevention of Cruelty to Animals.

costs on average $200 but can run as high as $400, depending on the practitioner. Often local shelters and rescue groups have several different veterinary practices they can recommend, so check to see if they have a list of providers.

The Best Friends dog application form asks how much the potential adopter is willing to pay for medical care. Options range from "up to $100" to "up to $5,000" and "whatever it takes." Consider the impact on your budget if an injury or illness occurs. If costs are high and your budget is tight, you should decide what you could afford to do *before* you adopt a dog. Know that, as a dog ages, his medical costs may increase or he may develop an illness, such as diabetes, that requires specialized care. Some successful budgeting strategies include keeping a separate credit card for a dog's medical emergencies. Some people have set aside money in a separate bank account solely for unexpected costs like these.

Living Spaces

Dogs need room to be dogs, and the amount of living space you have is an important factor to consider. First and foremost, find out if there are any pet restrictions in the lease for your apartment or the bylaws of your homeowners' association. Rental home contracts often prohibit pets or place a limit on their size. Make sure you are allowed to have a dog in your residence before you begin your search.

Indoors, you should have enough physical space to accommodate a dog. Apartments may not be right for Saint Bernards, although some large breeds adapt to indoor living because of their more sedentary lifestyle. Houses typically have more room, but they may not be perfect. Houses with fenced-in yards make bathroom breaks more convenient and offer a ready exercise space, but many homeowners without yards find ways to provide physical activities for their dogs.

A fenced-in yard is a huge bonus for a dog. A few dogs act as escape artists and are better off without boundaries to test, but in general, a fence allows a dog room to wander and relieve himself without you having to take him for a walk. Walking may be an acceptable solution in many cases, but there's always going to be a worst-case scenario. Would you want to put on your coat and shoes and walk your dog at two o'clock in the morning, during a pouring rainstorm, when she's got diarrhea?

You also should evaluate the spaces around your home. Can you walk your dog easily and safely in your neighborhood? Are there green spaces or dog parks nearby? Is there a veterinarian or kennel within easy driving distance, or someone who could watch the dog on short notice? Are you willing for your car to get dirty with dog hair and muddy paw prints?

All possibilities should be taken into account when deciding whether to adopt a dog. Surprises happen, which makes the commitment even more important.

Making Time

Companionship is a priority in most dog adoptions. It's fun to cuddle with a dog and watch television. But your dog is not a plush toy. She needs proper nutrition, physical exercise, and mental stimulation. Problems become inevitable if you don't have time or dedication to meet her needs. Dogs without exercise may get fat, listless, or hyperactive. Dogs without proper mental and physical stimulation may design their own brain- and bodybuilding games that may include tearing, chewing, barking, and digging.

"Bringing a dog into a home is a bargain, a promise, an agreement, a contract," Whitney says. "Your dog depends on you, the biped with the bigger brain, to make sure her basic needs are met."

Exercise is perhaps one of the most basic needs, as dogs' ancestors wandered great distances in search of food. Every dog, at every age, needs to be exercised every day. If your dog fails to get a proper workout, she's likely to exhibit behavioral problems that no amount of training will fix. A cat or fish may be a better fit for someone who can't be home enough to exercise a dog.

As you consider adopting a dog, ask yourself how much time you can devote to her physical health. Two half-hour exercise sessions each day are enough for most dogs. Others need more, especially puppies and dogs in the hunting, working, and herding groups. An energetic border collie, for example, almost certainly won't adjust happily to your lifestyle if you can give her only minimal exercise.

Providing different kinds of exercise brings a double bonus, stimulating muscles and brain. Dogs respond wonderfully to several types of exercise every day, such as playing tug, fetching a ball, and going on leash walks. (See Chapter 6 for some more creative ways you can exercise your dog's mind and body.)

Selecting a Dog: Getting Started

After you've decided a dog is right for you, you'll want to narrow your search. The following factors influence a smart decision.

Size: Small dogs have many benefits. They eat less and make smaller messes than do big dogs. They are likely to fit into virtually any person's living space. When it's time to walk them or take them to the vet, their small stature makes them physically more controllable—you can pick up a misbehaving Pekingese more easily than a 150-pound mastiff. But big dogs also have advantages. They're often less excitable and may be more likely to play well with children.

When considering size, make truthful assessments of your own physical abilities. Best Friends took in an extremely underweight shepherd named Bruno, who a senior citizen eventually adopted. She had to return him. As Bruno put on weight and regained his health, he became too strong for his new owner. Caregivers tell stories of other small-stature owners not being able to walk big dogs or take them to the vet. They urge applicants to be honest about their self-assessments and likelihood to successfully adopt a large dog. They compare the process to online dating services, which work best when you don't distort your own assets or lie about what you want in a date.

Energy Level: Some dogs prefer to take a jog, whereas others prefer to take a nap. Energy level is a big part of a dog's personality and her

Different Dogs, Different Needs Different kinds

of dogs have different needs, so consider how physical traits may impact your lifestyle when you start your adoption search. Dogs can be small, medium, or large: Can your household accommodate a larger dog? They can have shaggy, silky, or short coats: Can your budget handle the upkeep involved in a long-haired pooch?

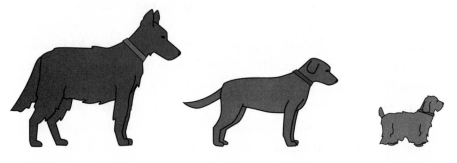

ability to fit into your home. Energy can be affected by many factors, but age and breed traits tend to be two of the most influential. If you've got plenty of time and energy to work with an energetic Jack Russell terrier, great. If not, perhaps a mellow basset hound is a better choice.

Manners: Your dog will need to be socialized so she remains comfortable when meeting new people and other dogs. If you want to care for a dog from a puppy, be prepared to introduce the dog to a hundred different people within the first few months of her life. If you're not in a position to provide this socialization or are too shy, consider adopting an older dog with a fuller set of social skills. Conversely, walking, training, and playing with a dog are great ways to meet other dog lovers and bring a shy person out of a shell. Don't forget your dog's individual personality. Dogs who avoid human contact will need to be conditioned to be around people; overly exuberant dogs will need to be taught to remain calm around people. Socialization is a never-ending process: Everyone, including your dogs, can always be improving manners.

Age: There are pluses and minuses to every age. Puppies require a huge time commitment from their owners because they demand constant attention. You'll need to work with puppies not only to socialize them, particularly to inhibit biting, but also to housetrain them and build proper behavior. If you do adopt a puppy, you have the advantage of not having to undo bad habits learned elsewhere. Another good thing about caring for a puppy is that she will grow up with other pets and people in the household, increasing the chances of their bonding. Still, if children are in the home, remember that children and puppies don't always mix well. Kids cannot always be counted on to perform puppy chores, or to remove temptations such as shoes and socks from where a puppy can get them. Adult dogs have the advantage of having passed through the difficult years of puppyhood and adolescence, although teenager-like behavior may continue well into middle age. Labrador retrievers often have longer adolescent periods than other breeds, for example. When adopting an adult dog, be aware that there's no guarantee that her behavior will or won't continue into old age. Older dogs have their own charms. They are still deserving of good homes even though they may have only a few months or years to live. That time can be rewarding for both of you. They usually have already been through the bumps of youth, including the perils of housetraining and the chewing stage. However, they may have higher medical bills than young dogs, and they may pass away soon after winning their owner's affections. An old dog may be the perfect fit for people who want a dog for only a short time, perhaps because they know they'll have a lifestyle change in a few years that will preclude dog ownership.

What's Breed Got to Do With It?

Humans are more than the sum of their genetic code, and so are dogs. The breed of a dog can tell you some general things about it: the color and type of coat, general size and weight, potential health issues, and what kind of activities the breed was designed to do. What it can't tell you is what a specific dog is like. You'll have to meet the dog to find that out!

Heredity may account for much of a dog's personality, but you can never be certain that a breed of dog you research online, in reference books, or by visiting a breed-specific rescue group will act like the profile constructed for her. Some retrievers don't like to chase balls. Some shih tzus don't like to sit on laps. Some Australian shepherds would just as soon cuddle as keep other animals in line.

Knowledge about a particular breed may then be beneficial in alerting you to types of behaviors or problems that have been catalogued in others, but it's not a blueprint for all members of that breed. That's not to downplay the importance of research into which of the many dog breeds or mixed breeds might be right for you. It is merely a cautionary tale against investing too heavily in stereotypes. Best Friends recommends getting to know individual dogs.

For years, commonly recognized breeds in the United States have often been divided into seven groups: sporting, working, herding, hound, terrier, toy, and a miscellaneous collection called non-sporting. Each has some common but not universal characteristics. About 25 percent of shelter dogs are purebred. The rest have the attributes of two or more breeds: They're called mixed breeds, or just plain lovable mutts.

Mutts: The mixed-breed dog, or mutt, has advantages and disadvantages over his purebred cousins. The biggest plus is genetic. Mixing bloodlines tends to dramatically reduce the incidence of gene-based diseases. "Hybrid vigor" is true not only of dogs but of all species. The evolutionary concept of the survival of the fittest begins with the idea of genetic variation resulting in selection of creatures best adapted to their environment. Inbreeding practically eliminates variance.

Mutts also are widely available, being far more common than any purebred dropped off at a shelter or rescue group. Their variety of size and shape lets you choose the dog for who he is, not for his conformity (or lack of it) to any set of purebred standards.

Mutts often are among the hardiest, smartest, and most unique dogs. If you know the mutt's ancestry, you might look for some combination of traits from the various breeds in the family tree. But there's no guarantee they will appear. If you don't know the dog's ancestry, you may have little idea of his eventual size and character.

You might not know how big a puppy will get, or how much grooming he might need. That means you need to be prepared for surprises. If they occur, they should not affect your love for your dog. You wouldn't disown your son, for example, just because he grew to be more than six feet tall and weigh more than 300 pounds.

Sporting Dogs: The sporting group typically includes spaniels, wirehaired pointers, golden and Labrador retrievers, setters, and Weimaraners. These dogs were chosen and bred over countless generations—an example of "artificial" instead of natural selection—to assist humans in hunting food for the table. Some are adept at pointing to hidden game. Others flush birds into the open. Some retrieve birds and game that have been shot. And some do all of these things. Because they have been bred to work closely alongside humans, they usually are loyal, affectionate, and quick to please.

Sporting breeds tend to be happiest when they get to spend a lot of time outside with their people. They usually get along with children because of the joy of active play. Success stories about adoptions of Labs and golden retrievers into families with children are common. Whitney recalls how Murphy, the Lab-golden mix her family adopted when she was a girl, happily endured whatever antic play the Jones' children devised. Murphy would consent to being dressed up, hitched to a wagon, and endlessly cuddled.

Care for dogs in the sporting group includes frequent brushings for the long-haired breeds, such as setters and spaniels. Grooming not only keeps the dogs looking nice but also reduces the amount of hair shed on furniture and carpets. Spaniels may be prone to eye problems as they age, and large breeds may suffer hip dysplasia. Surgery may be required to correct this misalignment of the leg joint if the dog is suffering pain. Other treatment options include weight loss, medication, and low-impact exercise such as swimming.

Working Dogs: The working group includes Akitas, boxers, Doberman pinschers, Great Danes, mastiffs, rottweilers, Saint Bernards, and Siberian huskies, in addition to many others. Humans selected and bred these dogs to perform particular tasks other than hunting animals and birds on land.

All breeds in this group have powerful muscles and do not tire easily. The Saint Bernard is a good example. True to the version seen on Saturday morning cartoons, he was bred in the Alps to find and rescue people trapped in snow. His large size and great strength help him push through deep drifts, and his powerful legs are good for digging or hauling. Others in the group were bred to swim, pull heavy weights, or guard livestock.

These dogs tend to want a job. If you're not likely to go hunting for lost skiers in the mountains, you might opt for extensive training as a way to keep your working dog occupied. These dogs tend to respond well to learning new commands, including tricks. Siberian huskies are bred to pull sleds, so they may try to pull hard on a leash and require more training than other dogs to train them out of that bad habit.

Typically outweighing other groups, working dogs often fit well into large houses that have ample yard space. However, their bulk tends to make them somewhat more sedentary than smaller breeds. That may make some of them a surprisingly good fit for smaller living spaces, provided they get plenty of exercise outdoors.

Some breeds, such as Saint Bernards, are known for heavy drool. Hip dysplasia and other joint injuries are not uncommon. The larger size of working dogs also increases the risk of them acquiring a condition called gastric dilatation-volvulus (GDV), or bloat, which causes the stomach to twist and swell, a medical emergency that requires swift care (in fact, any large breed dog from any group can suffer from this condition).

Herding Dogs: The herding group includes Australian shepherds, border collies, corgis, German shepherds, and Old English sheepdogs. Evolution has increased their desire to control the movement of other animals. They'll happily keep sheep or cattle from wandering. When there aren't any farm or ranch animals to corral, herding dogs may want to perform their innate skills on children or other humans. Some have been known to bump against kids, as if trying to corral them like sheep.

Their intelligence and desire to work and play hard make them a very visible group. German shepherds often serve as police dogs, and border collies often can be seen in city parks, racing again and again to snatch a flying disc out of the air. "With a border collie, typically speaking, you don't want to live in a studio apartment and have two jobs," Tamara says. "They need a job, and if you don't give them one, you will need to find other outlets for them—such as regular exercise, dog sports such as agility training or fly ball."

Herding dogs tend to be highly intelligent and active. Larger dogs in the herding group, like those in the working group, are at higher risk for GDV. They also are prone to hip dysplasia, which strikes more than 15 percent of German shepherds. That breed also has the most perianal fistulas, infected lesions that form near the anus. These inflammations are believed to affect German shepherds because they carry their thick tails near their bodies, restricting air circulation and allowing bacteria to flourish.

Hounds: The hound group includes Afghans, basenjis, bassets, beagles, bloodhounds, dachshunds, foxhounds, greyhounds, Irish wolfhounds, salukis, and whippets. Like the sporting group, hounds have been bred to seek wild game, albeit usually on the small side. For instance, dachshunds were bred small to fit into badger holes. Some breeds are especially adept at tracking over great distances by following the tiniest remnants of scent. Other breeds hunt by locking their eyes onto movement. These include basenjis and greyhounds, earning them the descriptive name sight hounds.

Hounds have two strong tendencies. The first is to track by smell or sight. This trait may have earned the group the unfair label of being stubborn. When a hound dog detects the scent of an animal and begins to track, the experience may overwhelm her other senses. Calling her away from the scent may be hard to do—not because she's willfully ignoring you, but because she is so totally focused on the information reaching her nose. Thus, many hounds aren't the best breed to take off leash while on a hike. They may run off to follow what they see or smell.

"I don't trust my sight hound off leash," Tamara says. "She wants to chase, and in her case, she wants to kill rabbits, chickens, and so on. I can do a lot of training, but I can never trust her 100 percent. Other dogs of mine are awesome off leash."

The second common characteristic to the hounds is their tendency to bay. Just as Elvis Presley sang, hound dogs may be "crying all the time." Left alone in an apartment, for example, a beagle or basset may sing a one-note song—*wooo! wooooo!*—over and over again. Although some dog owners appreciate the tune, neighbors might not be so enthusiastic.

Dysplasia occurs in the hound group but usually is not as big a problem as with larger dogs. Low-slung dogs such as basset hounds and dachshunds are more likely to develop back troubles from ruptured discs between their vertebrae.

Terriers: The terrier group includes the Airedale, cairn, fox, Jack Russell, miniature bull, Skye, and Welsh terriers, as well as miniature schnauzers. The group also includes a variety of dogs lumped under the name "pit bull." Also referred to as "bullies," the designation includes bull terriers, American Staffordshire terriers, and Staffordshire bull terriers. Although Airedales and some pit bulls can be physically imposing, other terriers tend to be on the small side, yet make up in heart what they might lack in stature.

Terriers are energetic, spunky, and alert. Bred to kill vermin, they tend to train easily, aim to please their owners, and can form the strongest of attachments. In the 19th century, a Skye terrier named Greyfriar's Bobby guarded the grave of his master for 14 years. When Bobby died at 16, his devotion was recognized by the erection of a statue in his honor in Edinburgh, Scotland.

The notion of bully breeds being innately vicious toward people is a myth based on their unfortunate association with dogfighting rings. Unless trained otherwise, pit bulls tend to bond closely with people and make good pets for children—"Petey" of the *Our Gang* movie series was a pit bull.

Of late, Jack Russells have become popular for adoption because of their high profile in movies and television shows, but they also have a high return rate. Although they command a loyal following, they tend to demand a lot of attention, have energy to burn, and are what Tamara calls "wicked smart." Jack Russells, like other terriers, tend to make the best pets when their owners engage in lots of activities with them.

Terrier coats do vary in length and texture, from the short hair of the bull terrier to the longer wiry coat of a Scottish terrier. The shorter-coated dogs tend to just need a weekly brushing and the occasional bath, whereas longer-haired dogs, especially those who do not shed, may require brushing a few times a week and a trim every few months.

Healthwise, certain breeds do have some things to watch out for. Pit bull terriers have heightened risk of cataracts, hip dysplasia, congenital heart disease, and allergies that affect the skin. All puppies should not be strenuously exercised until they are ten months old to avoid damaging their bones, but Skye terrier puppies may have an even higher tendency toward injury if physically challenged too soon in their lives.

Toy Dogs: The toy group includes Chihuahuas, Maltese, Pekingese, pugs, toy poodles, shih tzus, and Yorkshire terriers. As the name suggests, toys are tiny. But small does not necessarily mean low maintenance. They need as much exercise and training as larger dogs. They often are associated with apartment living because of their smaller size. They sometimes are housetrained to relieve themselves indoors in a litter box or on puppy pads, as their bowel movements are small and relatively easy to clean up and, if housed in a high-rise, they may not be able to reach the outdoors before nature takes its course. Still, they should be housetrained and taught good manners. Size should not determine whether or not a dog is well behaved.

Young children may be inclined to treat toy breeds like playthings because of their size. Parents should educate their kids that dogs can be feisty and resist being cuddled, turning defensive when they feel threatened. They also can get underfoot quite easily, causing a hazard for the elderly and the unaware. Many small dogs have been injured or killed by people stepping or tripping on them. Adults can also suffer injury when tripping over an unseen dog underfoot.

Grooming costs can vary for toy dogs, but they may need more frequent grooming than larger dogs. Common ailments include dental problems, which can be lessened with regular tooth brushing, and breathing difficulties linked to toys with brachiocephalic, or flat-nosed, skulls, like pugs or Pekingese (many large breed dogs are also brachiocephalic such as boxers and English bulldogs). Bone injuries from jumping off sofas and chairs, or from being stepped on, also are more common among toys than some other breeds.

Nonsporting Dogs: The nonsporting group includes bichon frises, Boston terriers, Lhasa apsos, miniature and standard poodles, bulldogs (including American, French, and English bulldogs), Dalmatians, and chow chows. These breeds don't neatly fit in the other groups and have been lumped into a catchall category. That makes it tough to link characteristics with the entire group. Instead, it's better to consider the breeds individually. For instance, the chow has a reputation for being serious and independent, whereas the bichon frise tends to be happy-go-lucky.

Care of these dogs also varies widely. Grooming of a standard poodle, whose hair grows but does not shed, requires regular trips to a doggie salon. The short-haired Boston terrier, on the other hand, just needs an occasional going over.

Diseases also vary, but the English bulldog may stand alone for having costly health problems. Narrow breeding lines have made this dog prone to heatstroke and breathing problems. Puppies may be active, but older dogs tend toward a sedentary lifestyle.

Upkeep

Check into the grooming requirements of the dog you're considering. In general, most dogs may need a weekly going over, based on their coat and activity level. If you live in a moist, warm climate, check your dog's skin regularly for fleas, ticks, and mites (consult your vet to see if your dog needs medications to keep from being bitten by these pests). Short-haired dogs, although not requiring regular trips to the groomer, do shed and will need more frequent grooming during shedding season (generally in the spring and fall). Long-haired dogs usually require more maintenance in brushing and in cleaning up after shedding. Long coats also are more likely to attract burrs and dust, so regular cleaning is important.

Dogs also need to have their teeth cleaned regularly to prevent gum disease and other illnesses. Dogs with longer ears (like setters, bloodhounds, and cocker spaniels) will need their ears inspected about once a week to make sure they are clean and free from infection. Your dog's nails will also need to be clipped (the frequency will depend on how much of the nail is worn down by the surfaces on which the dog walks). Keeping your dog groomed and clean isn't just cosmetic; a clean dog is a healthy dog as regular inspection of your dog's coat, skin, teeth, ears, and nails may clue you in to many health problems that may spring up.

Special Needs

Finally, you might consider adopting a dog with special needs. Dogs with fewer than four legs, dogs with medical conditions, incontinent dogs, blind dogs, deaf dogs—all deserve human companionship. Their challenges may require just a little extra attention, or ongoing therapy and veterinary care.

Some adopters seek special-needs dogs because they love a challenge or they feel sympathy for dogs others might consider defective. Despite such dogs' disabilities, they—like all dogs—respond to caregivers with unconditional love, inspiring admiration and joy. Adopters of special-needs dogs must make the same lifelong commitment as they would with any dog. They may realize, however, that some serious physical handicaps may make such a commitment shorter than most.

Wiggles, a buff-colored, bowlegged bulldog mix, seemed an unlikely candidate for adoption when he came to Best Friends in 2007 from the streets of California. As a result of a neurological disorder, he staggered when he walked and frequently fell over. He also had the indelicate habit of dropping scat at inopportune times.

To top it off, Wiggles had a goofy face: His lower jaw jutted too far forward to meet his upper teeth evenly, and only one of his ears pointed up. Nevertheless, even Wiggles found a forever home when a family from Colorado saw his picture on a website, drove to Best Friends to meet him, and decided to take him home—wiggly limbs, underbite, random poop, and all.

Every Dog Is an Individual

Remember that you can research yourself and your potential canine friend and still be pleasantly—or unpleasantly—surprised once you adopt. The puppy you fall in love with may grow into an adult of a size and personality you did not expect. The quiet adult dog you saw in his run may turn into a bundle of energy when he is in his new home. Do keep in mind that breed characteristics are just that—characteristics and generalizations that tend to run in a particular breed. The retriever who doesn't like to chase balls might curl up against your knees every night. The shih tzu who doesn't like to sit on your lap may enjoy chasing the ball for hours.

Just because a dog isn't what you thought he was at first doesn't mean that he doesn't have great qualities of his own or that you won't have amazing experiences together. You can encourage some behavior by finding positive ways to motivate your dog into activities that you can both enjoy. Every dog is a product not only of genetics but of individual personality, training, and life circumstances. If you can let go of your initial expectations and value your new companion for who he is, you just might enjoy the most fulfilling relationship of your life.

Top Tips

•When you adopt a dog, you are making a lifelong commitment.

•Before you start actively searching for a new dog, start with yourself first. Do an honest self-assessment of your personality and lifestyle. Consider why you want a dog. What is the reason you're thinking of adopting? Do you have the time and resources that a dog will need?

•Is your family ready for the responsibility of a dog? Is it something that everyone wants? How will your other pets handle a new addition?

•Think about your budget. Can you afford it? What about emergency expenses?

•Consider the future. Make sure your life will allow for a dog in the long term as well as the present.

•Size, energy, personality, upkeep, and age are all important things to consider when trying to find the right dog for you.

•Don't try to replace a pet you have recently lost. Every dog is different; expecting the new one to fill the old one's shoes isn't fair and will likely leave you disappointed.

•All dogs are individuals. Breed history can give you some insight into potential behaviors and health issues, but it is not a concrete blueprint for what your dog will be like.

When meeting a dog for the first time, she'll most likely use her nose to check you out—just like Clover who greets the camera with a curious sniff.

Canine
Communication

Pat Whitacre is convinced he could have won a big pot of money on television with a home video of Cactus Jake, an Australian cattle dog mix.

Cactus Jake weighed less than 40 pounds, but he could look pretty scary behind a gate. Whitacre, a certified professional dog trainer at Best Friends, remembers approaching Cactus Jake's run at the Maggie's Mercantile neighborhood of Dogtown a few years ago.

"He was very intimidating," Pat says. "If you walked within ten feet of his gate, he would bark, throw himself at the gate, and grab it with his teeth. He would shake it, foaming at the mouth."

Then, Pat opened the gate and went inside.

"Suddenly he's down on all fours and acting like my best friend. I stepped out." It was as if Cactus Jake was two dogs: displaying anger and aggression to Pat on one side of the gate, and friendliness on the other.

Given the behavior Cactus Jake was presenting, it would have ordinarily required an emergency for Pat to walk into such a run. The difference this time was that Cactus Jake's caregivers had given Pat a consistent detailed history of his behaviors toward people in and out of his run.

"You could go in and out ten times in a row," Pat says. "His behavior never changed. He went from a terrifying 'Cujo' dog, to 'Pet me, I'm your buddy.' All you had to do was step through that magic barrier. It was like a light switch, how he changed—on/off, on/off."

Then there's Nochi, who appears to be just the opposite.

"He's conflicted," says Sherry Woodard, Best Friends' resident animal behavior consultant. "People expect him to be something he's not. He's little and appears to be easygoing and happy. He solicits attention as people approach him."

Nochi, a little gray mix featured in the National Geographic television series *DogTown,* has difficulty with trust. He loves trainer John Garcia, but he's not about to give away his love to strangers. Nochi gives plenty of signs of inviting closeness from people he doesn't know, including wagging his tail and looking relaxed. But when strangers get too close to him, Nochi feels overwhelmed and tries to scare them away.

Some dogs at Best Friends, like Nochi, seem to solicit human contact but then make it abundantly clear that they have mixed feelings about meeting new people. Others like Cactus Jake have a scary bark but welcome the approach of humans.

Some dogs may roll over on their backs to show their chest and stomach, but react negatively when a human misinterprets the action as an invitation to a belly rub. Those dogs may be revealing their undersides to indicate they pose no threat and would like an intruder to go away. When a visitor misreads the intended communication and reaches closer to pat the seemingly submissive dog, she may snap and bite.

Complicated? Absolutely. As complicated as the multitude of variables that go into any form of communication. Just as the meaning of words said aloud can vary depending on tone, vocal stress, body language context, and other factors collectively known as *prosody*—you can say, "Love," and mean a variety of things—dogs communicate with signals that can have multiple meanings, change rapidly, and be specific to the situation.

An understanding of canine communication is a good beginning to any relationship with a dog. An exact translation isn't always possible, but it is good to consider what the dog *might* be saying. For one thing, a wagging tail isn't always the sign of a happy dog—it can signify many different moods: happiness, fear, anxiety, or something else entirely. For another, some dogs are difficult to read if they have cropped ears or tails, faces hidden behind long hair, or fur that always stands at attention.

Yet, it is possible—even vital—for a dog owner or prospective owner to try to learn the basics of what a dog is trying to

Grumpy Old Dogs

Aging may complicate a dog's behavior. Aches and pains that come with growing old often contribute to undesirable behaviors. Old dogs with chronic pain, such as arthritis, may be more sensitive to handling and unable to do some things they used to. If your dog's behavior changes at any age or you notice physical changes or signs of pain, schedule an appointment with your veterinarian. An old dog may also develop dementia, which could bring on dramatic changes in personality.

say. Becoming familiar with the multiple meanings of tail wags, averted gazes, and other signals will help provide a better understanding of what a dog is trying to communicate, his mood, his comfort in a given situation, and his reaction to changes in his environment. It is a skill that will help in selecting a dog, make training more efficient, and avoid some (but not all) unpleasant misunderstandings. While reading a chapter in a book may be useful in getting you started, it is no substitute for experience gained from watching how dogs interact with other dogs and with people. So, take the following caveat to heart: Don't treat any of the descriptions of dog behavior offered here or anywhere else as ironclad laws. They must remain mere guidelines because dogs, like people, are all different. Treating them otherwise because you believe you are an expert on dog behavior could be an invitation to a bad bite. Even dogs can misread other dog signals. If you err, do so on the side of caution.

"Reading a dog's body language is a little bit like predicting the weather," Pat says. "Only it's without tools like Doppler radar, and without information of what a storm did three counties to the west of you." In other words, there are tendencies and trends, but no perfect predictions.

Besides the risk of drawing incorrect conclusions, humans face the difficulty of judging something that can change rapidly. When you look at drawings or snapshots of dog behavior, you may think the image correctly captures a dog's mood. However, behavior is fluid. A dog may be feeling joy one second and fear the next. Always be careful. A dog may not have decided to bite until a split second before he does—and not nearly enough time for you to read the signals and get out of the way.

"To study their behavior in real time, volunteer at a local shelter and go to a dog park," Sherry says. "Watch all different kinds of dogs. Get to know dogs. Each one has a personality. What motivates them, what they want."

Whole Body Language

If you want to begin to assess a dog's mood, you can do so from far away. Sherry's single best piece of advice is to look at the whole dog at once and observe how the dog holds her body. Is the dog loose and wiggly, as when she relaxes and does something she enjoys, or tight and stiff, as when she is taken against her will to a veterinarian's office? Loose, wiggly dogs are probably more open to a human's approach or contact than are tight, stiff ones. But even that generalization isn't a sure bet. Seemingly relaxed dogs sometimes bite, and stiff ones sometimes melt into the most pleasant of companions.

Sherry takes a stroll through some of the dusty streets of Dogtown to point out examples of whole-body language. There's Batgirl, a stout-chested black terrier mix rescued from New Orleans after Hurricane Katrina. Named for her batlike ears that point like the caped crusader's cowl, she shivers and wiggles with excitement in her enclosure, with her tongue hanging out in a big smile and her ears relaxed as Sherry approaches. Batgirl moves with a floppy, goofy grace that seems to say, "I'm comfortable." Then there's Tweed, a mostly white mix of Australian cattle dog and border collie with some other breeds perhaps thrown in. He barks and whines as Sherry draws near. He approaches the fence that separates him from Sherry, and then stiffly backs away. All the while, his nose twitches; he smells the air, looking for clues to tell him what's going on. Tweed's stiffness from tail to nose indicates that his mood is stressed and anxious, the opposite of Batgirl's. Finally, there's Jango, a mixed breed with trust issues. Jango wags and acts loose and wiggly when you are at a safe distance, but—*snap!*—when you cross an invisible line in the red Utah dirt, he becomes tense, aggressive, and loud. A dog's whole body can give you a quick read of where the dog is at in that particular moment, but individual parts can reveal more details about where he might be going.

Body Parts

When looking for indicators of mood, parts of the dog can tell you a lot. In addition to the dog's overall body looseness, you'll want to consider the ears, eyes, mouth, posture, fur, and tail. Each element may convey many emotions, so it's best to gather as much information as possible to make your best guess about what a dog is feeling.

Ears: Looking at a dog's ears sometimes may signal what's happening in the space between them, the brain. Dogs with ears that hang low or ears that have been cropped may be harder to read than those with upright ears, but they still may give some indication of mood.

Ears that sit upright and point forward may indicate a dog who is alert and interested in something. When accompanied by a head tilt, perked-up ears may mean the dog finds something curious—or incomprehensible. The dog may be trying to figure out the situation.

In general, relaxed ears may indicate a dog is feeling calm, but if the ears turn sharply down or backward and whether or not the dog growls, he may be suspicious, fearful, or anxious. The actual meaning will depend on the dog, and if you are unfamiliar with him, it's best to proceed slowly and with caution if the ears are held in this position. "If a dog puts his ears down and growls at me, I may know that with a particular dog, I can go up and pet him and it will be OK," Pat says. "But with a dog I don't know, I say, 'This is a dog who appears uncomfortable.' I don't want to make the matter worse by intruding more on his space and approaching closer."

Such a dog probably just wants you to go away, and could even see your actions as threatening. Many nervous dogs grow even more anxious when you speak to them, even in a soothing voice. Some are so frightened that they don't want you to speak at all. "I have had dogs get up and bolt as soon as I said, 'That's a good doggie,'" Pat says.

Eyes: Eyes are perhaps the most expressive part of the human face, and dogs' eyes should not be overlooked. Eyes can reveal subtle differences in mood. A relaxed dog is likely to have what Sherry calls "soft" eyes. There's no obvious sign of tension; the dog's easy gaze is part of an overall relaxed, loose posture. Dogs don't have eyebrows, but some of the skin above a dog's eyes may raise or drop like a human eyebrow. As with humans, raised "eyebrows" may indicate interest, whereas lowered brows may mean the dog is uncertain. Dogs may relax their faces when feeling affection around a human they love, causing their lids to partially close and their eyes to peek out from half-closed slits.

On the other hand, a focused, stiff gaze, especially when paired with a tense body posture and other signals in the ears, fur, and tail, may add up to a dog feeling defensive and vulnerable.

Hair Gets in Your Eyes Remember that a dog's eyes won't tell you anything if you can't see them. Sheepdogs and other breeds with cascades of hair over their faces may be harder to analyze than short-haired dogs or long-haired varieties who have been trimmed.

Dogs know the power of eye-to-eye communication. If two dogs meet, they may look at each other's eyes, then should look away to defuse any threat or challenge. Unless socialized to accept a human's affectionate gaze, a dog likely will interpret a person's fixed stare as a challenge and a possible threat. If you don't know a particular dog's personality, avoid staring into his eyes.

Mouth: As with other parts of the body that reveal a dog's mood, the mouth is complicated. A dog may wrinkle his nose and expose his teeth in what could be a happy grin, or it could also be a sign of discomfort, submission, or a warning that he is about to bite. This display may or may not be paired with a growl or other vocalization.

When under stress, a dog may use his mouth to exhibit "displacement" behaviors. These are activities that are normal at other times, such as yawning when sleepy. However, yawning when not tired, in any situation in which a dog might feel uncomfortable, would seem out of place. Displacement behaviors occur most often during moments of stress or anxiety, and may serve as physical methods by which a dog calms himself.

A dog's displacement behaviors involving the mouth include:

- licking the lips when the dog has not been eating or drinking.
- exhaling a breath, with a puff that moves the lips, sometimes while looking away or whining.
- yawning when exposed to a new situation or in an emotional context.
- open-mouthed panting when the dog is not overheated.
- drooling, especially among dogs who don't normally drool.

Posture: As previously noted, an overall posture that is loose and wiggly is likely a good sign of a relaxed and happy dog, whereas a stiff body posture points to the opposite conclusion. "There is certainly a softness in a dog who is comfortable," Sherry says. "If the dog is not comfortable, you may not see much looseness at all. You'll see a dog that is slowing down, or not coming toward you, or coming toward you while up on her toes and looking anxious and somewhat stiff."

Freezing is a good indication of a dog feeling something is not right. When a dog's body grows still from nose to tail, for even the briefest moment, she's telling you she is scared, feels cornered, or is trying to guard something. Slow your own body down in response, and be aware that in this moment the dog is making a decision about what to do next and may be considering several options, including whether or not to bite.

Rolling over often means a dog is trying to diffuse a tense situation, but to be confident that such is the case you will need to know the dog and watch all of the dog's body. A loose tail and mouth, with the lips loose, likely mean the dog is asking for a belly rub. But a tucked tail, combined with a stiff mouth, may be just the opposite. A dog also may seem to solicit attention by exhibiting a relaxed posture and rolling on her back, when all she is really saying is, "I don't want any trouble," and then snap when a person gets too close.

A dog also may stamp her front legs while keeping her back legs planted. This often is a sign of excitement, but this could be either a challenge or an indication of wanting some attention.

Whole-body displacement behaviors can be seen in stressful situations. A dog who feels anxiety might shake off, move away, pace, or circle after being handled. During an overly rough session of play with another dog, she might lie on the ground either because she is tired or she wants to reduce the level of activity.

Fur: The technical term for when a dog's hair stands up is *piloerection*. It is especially noticeable on the back and shoulders of short-haired dogs. A dog's hairs rising erect may offer the same advantage as when a puffer fish puffs: A body covered with erect hair looks larger than a body with flattened fur. The bigger the animal, the scarier it may appear to other animals, and that may scare off a potential threat. However, piloerection may not occur under control of the voluntary nervous system and may not even be done with any intent to look larger.

Piloerection may not mean a dog is getting ready to attack. It only indicates the heightened state of arousal, which could manifest itself in several ways. It often is associated with fear, but it could also indicate a state of happy arousal and excitement.

Long or matted hair can interfere with attempts to interpret piloerection. Beware of trying to read the mood of a dog with lots of very long hair. A sheepdog, for example, may have so much hair that it's difficult if not impossible for an observer to get a fix on his eyes, mouth, and ears.

Tail: A wagging tail can mean many things, so don't rely on reading the tail separate from the rest of a dog's body. Tail wagging could indicate anything from arousal to agitation, depending on the context.

Look not only at whether the tail is wagging, but also at how high or low the dog carries it. Then keep looking; the tail may change its motions in response to how close you get to the dog or how you act.

A tail that wags in a loose manner between high and low may suggest a dog is friendly and relaxed.

If the tail wags but hangs low, the dog may be communicating that he is afraid or unsure of a situation.

A tail that stands high and wags stiffly, like a metronome, could mean the dog is unsure, just like the dog whose tail droops while wagging. It also could mean he is scared or agitated, but not submissive. Sherry says, "If the dog's body is stiff, he is staring, and his ears are up, use caution. Moving away may keep you and the dog out of trouble—he may be about to make a bad decision."

When curled under and tucked between the legs, especially when paired with ears pulled back against the head, a tail may indicate a dog in fear, discomfort, or uncertainty. That doesn't necessarily mean the dog is about to bite, although that's a possibility. If it occurs in multiple situations, it may mean the dog lacks confidence, a behavioral issue that can be addressed and possibly improved through training.

Pat notes that humans may read a dog tucking her tail as a communication of fear. However, the dog may not be attempting to communicate that at all; instead, the tucking of a tail could be an involuntary physical response hardwired into the dog's neural pathways. Pat uses the analogy of people blushing when they feel embarrassed. Others who see the reddening of the skin may interpret it as a sign of embarrassment. However, the blusher did not choose to blush as a form of emotional communication. They may desperately wish they weren't visibly embarrassed. Likewise, dogs may exhibit physiological reactions involuntarily. Tucking the tail offers some protection to the vulnerable underbelly and may persist solely as a valuable survival mechanism in dangerous situations. That's another reason Pat cautions against interpreting what we can see as an attempt to communicate with us: Much of it is not intended to "say" anything at all.

"In one sense, the up-and-down movement of the tail can be read as an indicator of arousal," Pat says. "A high, erect tail does not always mean a dog is confident. But it does mean he is alert and on cue. As it gets lower, he may be more nervous and fearful. When it is fully tucked, a dog is often feeling a lot of stress.

From top to bottom, at no position can we definitely say the dog is relaxed or angry."

Dog Talk

Dogs communicate through vocal sounds as well as body language. Yet many owners try to make their dogs give up barking, whining, and growling. If dogs are denied the opportunity to make noise, they lose a valuable tool of communication. When dogs growl at Dogtown, the staff members say, "Thank you for telling me you are uncomfortable," and look for the cause. They would rather the dog communicate fear vocally than go straight to a more physical response with little warning.

Barking: Dogs don't need to bark all the time, and human neighbors probably don't want to hear it very much either. So owners should help their dogs to use their barks in ways acceptable to a world they share with people. Natural reasons for barking (that may not always be appreciated by humans) include:

Alert barking. Dogs bark in a state of arousal when they hear or see something unusual. Dogs are animals, and they use this behavior to alert others to something new. Many owners don't mind if a dog alerts them to a stranger in their yard or at the door.

Attention barking. Dogs bark to ask for something. For example, they may bark because it's their usual time to be fed or played with, or they need to go outside to relieve themselves. An attention bark at the back door a few hours after the dog has drunk a bowlful of water is appreciated.

Boredom barking. Dogs who don't get enough mental or physical stimulation may bark for something to do. When an owner enriches a dog's world with toys, chews, and walks, he likely will bark less.

Fearful barking. Dogs bark when they've been frightened, perhaps to tell another animal to keep its distance. This kind of barking may occur more often when a dog is on leash, backed into a corner, or has limited options to move away.

Playful barking. Dogs often bark when having a good time with other dogs. The pitch of a happy bark is usually higher than a bark sounded in fear or alert. Look for this kind of bark with a loose, wiggly dog with relaxed ears and mouth.

Growling: Growling, like barking, may communicate many things. Although usually associated with stress and fear, growling can be a part of play. Sherry knows many chow chow mixes who growl as part of their normal communication. Keep in mind the situation when you hear a growl—if you and your dog are engrossed in a good game of tug, a growl may be part of the game. If a growl comes when you approach a dog while she's eating, it's more likely a warning to stay back.

Growling could communicate a warning, perhaps indicating that a dog wants something to begin or to end. The dog may want to communicate his anxiety over an invasion of his space or a threat to his possessions. A dog who growls while baring teeth and stiffening is sending a clear message of feeling uncomfortable and possibly preparing to bite.

Still, Pat knows there is tremendous variability. He keeps a dog in his office who lifts her lip and shows her teeth at everybody who comes near. She pairs the mouth signals with an intimidating growl. Yet he can't recall her ever biting anybody.

"So, if people think her growling is a warning that she is going to bite, they would be getting the wrong information," he says.

Whining: Whining can be even more difficult to figure out. Sometimes a dog whines as a form of request. The whine signifies he wants to go out, to play with another dog, to get a handout from the table, or maybe to have access to somewhere he has been kept from going. Whining also can extend into signs of stress and anxiety.

To figure out why your dog whines, watch her behavior closely and try to look for correlations between whining and the situation at hand. What's going on before the start of the whining or as the whining continues? Where is the dog, and what does she want? When does it stop? What makes it stop? It could range from a request to do something fun to a sign that the dog is in pain. Undesired behaviors that defy explanation may be a reason to take a dog for a medical checkup.

Moods

Now that you've examined the parts that make up a dog's body language and the noises dogs make, try to piece them together into a larger whole. As with human speech, keep in mind that what's being communicated is often more than the sum of its parts.

Dogs' bodies may indicate they feel relaxed, aroused, playful, fearful, stressed, or threatened. Or they may even be confused and give off confused signals.

Relaxed: Sherry keeps a photograph of a relaxed dog on a Web page where she posts tips about reading a dog's body language. The gray-and-white male terrier mix has rolled on his back to allow a woman to rub his chest. He holds his right front leg in the air in a loose arc toward her. His back legs lie lightly against the ground. His eyes are half-closed in delight and his mouth has flopped open, revealing a loose tongue. All told, he is giving classic signs of being relaxed and content with his loose behavior.

Eyes, ears, tail, mouth, and hair—all are likely to show signs of softness when a dog feels relaxed. Body posture should appear natural. A confident dog is likely to hold head and tail high, with ears either erect or relaxed, and have a relaxed gaze.

If a dog's body becomes stiff, be careful. A dog who freezes up probably is not comfortable or open to interaction with a human or another dog.

Aroused: Arousal indicates only an enhanced alertness. It does not necessarily mean that what follows is a desirable or undesirable behavior. A tail may be held high when a dog is relaxed, but it also could indicate a heightened state of arousal. Other possible signs of arousal include ears being held stiff and forward, hackles rising, mounting behavior, and vocalizing.

An aroused dog may stand stiff, taking in every detail of his environment. Or he may paw, mouth, or jump up, perhaps trying to solicit attention.

Arousal may cause changes in a dog's normal behavioral routines. When a dog's body goes on high alert, it's because something in his environment triggered the release of adrenaline into his bloodstream. Blood flow gets diverted to the muscles and the sensory organs, and away from anything not needed for the fight-or-flight response. That includes the digestive system. A dog who is highly aroused or stressed probably won't take a food treat, even though he normally loves them.

Dog Moods

A dog's body language changes as his mood does. Note how different a dog's ears, tail, mouth, and posture change with his state of mind.

Relaxed

Body is loose with natural posture. Eyes, ears, tail, and mouth should all appear open and calm.

Aroused

Body can be stiff. Tail may be held high. Ears are erect and forward. Gaze is focused.

Playful

Loose, wiggly body. Tail is high and wagging loosely. Mouth is open and relaxed. May execute a "play bow" by putting hindquarters in the air and lowering the front.

Stressed/Fearful

Body is stiff and may be crouched low to the ground. Tail may be tucked underneath body. Ears are back and down.

Stressed: Stress manifests itself with opposite extremes of behavior. A dog feeling stress undergoes changes that may cause greater or lesser activity. A stressed dog may exhibit hyperactivity, pacing and pawing, vomiting, coughing, sneezing, yawning, shaking, whining, leaving damp footprints from sweating, or running away—or some combination of those and other signs of excitement. Or he may shut down, freezing in place, backing away from activity, hiding, or refusing to eat, drink, or play. In addition, signs that may point to stress also could be part of normal behavior, such as drooling or barking. Boredom also can contribute to stress and may result in a dog chewing or tearing objects around the house.

A dog probably feels stress and fear when she starts to whine, paces back and forth or in circles, exhibits unusual drooling, or tucks her tail and moves away. In addition to the displacement behaviors described earlier in the chapter, a stressed-out dog may scratch herself even though she doesn't itch; look away when another dog or a person walks toward her; or start to growl (although growls can mean many things).

When you see that a dog you are interacting with is experiencing stress, stop whatever you are doing. Slow your movements and think about what is going on. Try to figure out what is causing the stress so you do not add to it in the short run and can help improve the dog's coping skills in the long run.

Causes of stress may include a startle, sounds, places, and people; odd behaviors among those near the dog; poor diet, lack of exercise, or mental stimulation; and hidden physical problems that might require a veterinarian's attention.

As stress increases, a dog may escalate toward signs associated with fear and threatening behavior. This may include snarling, growling, and lifting of the lips. These are only active signs; if a dog is more passive, he may withdraw or shut down and try to become "invisible."

Fearful: A stiff dog is often a fearful dog. If a dog's entire body goes rigid, take it as a sign that he wants the rest of the world to slow down too. A fearful dog may instinctively try to protect his belly by lowering himself toward the ground or tucking his tail. He also may move his ears back, out of harm's way.

Moving too fast around such a dog may invite getting bit. Stiffness also appears as a likely indicator of fear in a tight pattern of tail wagging, a frozen stare, and erect ears. Fearful dogs require caution. Do not stare into their eyes. Move away—if you were the cause of the dog's fear, you may have invaded his personal space or made a move the dog interpreted as a threat. You may see the dog's body language change as you move away.

Some fears are extremely difficult to pinpoint and thus to treat. "Dogs have emotions. They are individuals, and we don't always know why they feel what they do," Sherry says. "We often have very little information about a dog's past. They may perceive things differently than we do. Something in the past may have scared the dog, and some current event may reawaken those feelings."

She recalled being bewildered by a dog named Miles, a nine-pound dog whose mother was a purebred Chihuahua and father was unknown. Miles would try to bite when Sherry would try to hand him from her arms to another person. For a long time, she couldn't figure out why he grew agitated when she passed him to someone else.

As Sherry searched her memory, she traced the likely reason for Miles's behavior to an incident when he was a puppy. Miles was only three days old and in precarious health when she took charge of his care. Sherry constantly poked him with needles to give him fluids intravenously and, when he was older, started him on a series of vaccinations.

When it came time for a third round of shots and the insertion of an identifying microchip, Sherry handed Miles to a vet tech, who gave the dog his vaccinations and then inserted the microchip with a 10-gauge needle—big enough to cause a memorable sting. Sherry deduced that, after that experience, Miles associated being handed to another person with the pain he remembered from feeling the giant needle. To begin to get Miles to make positive associations, she began handing him to people who gave him a treat and handed him back.

Threatened: When a dog curls his lips to bare his teeth, wrinkles the skin on his nose, growls, and snaps at the air, he's probably giving a clear message that he will have no choice but to resort to violence if he's not left alone. But that doesn't mean that all bites are preceded by such signs. When people have been bit, they've usually been surprised. They didn't see the normal signs, often because they let down their guard and didn't continually monitor the behavior of a seemingly docile dog.

A threatening dog generally has a stiffness to his body. He may growl and bare his teeth, staring with a fixed, intense glare at any-one he perceives as a possible threat. And the hair on his back may rise as a sign of the fight-or-flight response.

Confused: Finally, the dog may be confused. She may be troubled by something she has never encountered before and not know how to react. She may show her confusion through mixed signals, such as pairing a growl with an apparently loose wag, for example. Or she may be confused by the mixed signals she receives from the humans around her.

The best thing you can do is not to assume a dog's behavior can mean only one thing. By paying close attention, you may be able to identify some of the behaviors a dog might choose but not predict the exact course of action she'll take. If you're not prepared for all of her potential reactions, don't do anything suddenly. If you make a move toward a dog and she appears nervous, don't press the issue. Take note of how the dog reacted, and back away. Proceed only when you can do so safely.

Your Own Body Language

Communication is a two-way street. Your dog is watching you for signs that he tries to interpret. Your own demonstration of calm, happy behavior will be understood to some degree. Just remember to act in ways with which both you and the dog are comfortable.

"We are not dogs ourselves, so don't mimic dog behavior," Sherry says. She once observed an adult Dogtown intern crawling across the floor on her hands and knees in a room with several dogs. "I asked her, 'What are you doing?' She said, 'They can relate to this.' I said, 'Get up. That is not normal behavior at all. They know our normal behavior.'"

It's important to watch a dog as she reacts to your own body language.

"People don't realize when they move fast, when they're loud, or that they sometimes move their arms all over the place," Sherry says. "They sometimes lean over a dog. They approach head on. And they scare the dog, quite often."

She recommends controlling your body language to make yourself seem less threatening to a dog. Check your pace and your energy level before entering a dog's personal space. Act naturally and calmly. You also can make yourself seem less threatening by turning sideways to show a smaller profile to the dog. "The moment we make ourselves smaller, dogs read it as less of a threat," Sherry says.

Don't stare; look away from the dog's eyes to avoid implying a challenge. Don't try to put your hands on a dog right away, no matter what the dog's posture. Watch carefully for signs of the dog feeling at ease. Let the dog approach you if she is willing. There is no need to offer a hand; allow the dog to examine you without that added distraction.

Don't reach to pet a dog until you feel certain the action is welcome. If you wish to pet another person's dog, ask permission of the owner first. If the owner says OK, then you must essentially ask the same question of the dog. If the dog permits it, you may begin by stroking gently along the sides or neck with short motions in the direction of the dog's hair growth. A brief pet is a sufficient greeting for an unfamiliar dog. Do not grab the dog's tail. Watch the dog's

Looking to You Dogs communicate primarily through body language, and look to yours. When you shout, flail your arms, and stomp to show your anger at something your dog has done wrong, such as emptying a garbage can, your dog won't understand the lecture you give him. He will, however, read your actions as threatening. If you stay rigid with anger, your dog will see you as a continuing threat.

Knowing that your dog is watching your body language, you should be aware of how you move when you are around your dog. Think about not only the words you say, but also how you say them. If you and your dog are relaxed and having fun during training, you will both be eager for more.

reactions and prepare to move away if you see any signs of stress or fear.

If the dog welcomes the stroking, she may guide you to where she wants to be rubbed by moving against your hand. Dogs have different favorite places for a good scratch and pet; conversely, they also have different places where they may not like to be touched. Some dogs don't like to be rubbed near their ears; others don't enjoy being petted on top of their heads. Many dogs may adjust their heads beneath your fingers until you're scratching just the right sweet spot.

Misunderstandings

One last note: Don't expect dogs to communicate their moods perfectly. Dogs, like people, may not know what they're feeling at first. Their emotions may change. They may become confused. They may lack certain skills from being undersocialized. They may have negative associations due to past experiences, which may lead to miscommunications with humans. Whether meeting a dog for the first time or interacting with a dog you've known forever, be observant. Pay attention to the dog's body language, any vocalizations, and any new or different circumstances that could affect the encounter.

If you do have an encounter that leads to a bite or near bite, try to remember what happened just prior to the event. A dog who does bite may give only the briefest of signals beforehand. Therefore, it's important to note, and log, every detail of what occurred before the bite, including the dog's physical actions, the other people or animals present, the location, and what was happening, in order to work on understanding, improving, or managing the dog's behavior in the future. Remember, those cues from a particular dog cannot be generalized to others.

For instance, Pat cautions that our expectations can color how we read a dog. He tells the story of a Katrina rescue dog named Hobo Mississippi to illustrate the point. He was a hard dog to describe. Hobo Mississippi had the color pattern of a collie, combining tan, white, and gray markings, but with fluffy hair and a look that was part husky and part sheltie, packed onto about 50 solid pounds. Pat says he met Hobo Mississippi at a staging area after the hurricane rescue. The dog was one of the last seven or eight who were taken from the storm-devastated Gulf Coast to Best Friends.

"We were pretty good buddies down in Mississippi," Pat says. "Because I knew him, I was working with him. And I thought I would see what he knew."

He took a pouch full of treats into the dog's run every day, always eliciting a wiggly, happy response. Pat lured Hobo Mississippi into a sit by manipulating the treat above the dog's head and then rewarded him. The dog mastered that behavior, and Pat wondered if he knew other skills. He thought he would try to get Hobo Mississippi to lie down. But, in retrospect, Pat knows he did a few things wrong.

"So I asked him to do a down," Pat says. "He had done two or three sits before I started to lure him into a down. He didn't understand what I wanted. So, I presented the lure, a couple of times, and then in an instant, he reached forward, snapped, bit me on the hand, and shook it. He did some pretty mean bites for a little guy."

Later, Pat realized his mistakes. First, he forgot that any dog trainer must be ready for any outcome of a training session, success or failure. He did not wear gloves, as he normally does for training exercises, because he had come to believe he didn't need them around Hobo Mississippi. Pat let his expectations of how difficult the requested task was cloud his interpretation of the signals the dog was giving. From the dog's perspective, Pat did everything he had done in previous visits, yet he withheld the treat for no reason. Pat held out the treat, as always. Hobo Mississippi sat, as always. And then, the dog got no treat. From the dog's point of view, he had been teased and denied an expected reward. Pat was watching the physical signals but he had misinterpreted them completely.

Knowing physical sounds and signs associated with dogs' moods and behaviors will increase your chances of finding a dog who's a good fit for you, your family, and your lifestyle when you visit an animal shelter, while reducing chances of an unpleasant encounter. Be on your own good behavior, and get your communication with a prospective "forever friend" off to a slow, easy start.

Top Tips

•Dog communication is not an exact science. Every dog is different; specific communication tendencies will vary from dog to dog and situation to situation.

•Context is everything. For instance, growls and barks can be warnings or parts of a game, so be sure to take the situation into account when assessing what the dog may be trying to tell you.

•A dog's posture is a strong indicator of his overall state. Loose, wiggly dogs tend to be relaxed and more accepting of an approach, whereas stiff, rigid dogs tend to be on alert and less welcoming of an encounter.

•Volunteer at your local shelter and visit dog parks to make firsthand observations of the broad range of dog behaviors. Observing dogs in action is a great way to learn how they communicate with people and with other dogs.

•A dog may convey emotion through his posture, fur, ear and tail position, as well as through his mouth and eyes. Look at all the body parts together when trying to assess mood.

Dogs of all ages—from puppies like these to adults and seniors—are available for adoption from animal control, animal shelters, and rescue groups.

The Search Begins

Once you've made the decision to bring a dog into your life, it's time to begin your search for your new dog. After doing honest self-assessment of your lifestyle, your budget, and your resources (as outlined in Chapter 1), your search can start. You've got a strong idea of what you're looking for, of how the other members of your household will participate in the dog's care, of the size, age, and energy level of your potential pet. This preliminary sketch is a great asset as you head out to adopt your dog.

So where do you begin to look? Luckily there are many great resources out there for people looking to adopt dogs. Local animal control facilities, privately funded animal shelters, rescue groups, and reputable online resources have plenty of amazing dogs who are waiting for you to come and start your relationship.

Adoptable Dogs

Your self-assessment should have given you an idea of what kind of dog you think would be the best match for your home and lifestyle. Use it to guide your search. It will not only help you find the right type of dog, it can also help you find the best places to look. At each one, you'll find an incredibly diverse group of dogs from which to choose. Mutts and purebreds; puppies and seniors; long hairs, short hairs; small, medium, and large dogs: You name it, and chances are, you can find it.

Twenty years ago, dogs surrendered to shelters likely faced euthanasia within a few days unless someone took them home. Today, the situation has improved: As many as three-quarters of all dogs given up for adoption find new homes. That still leaves 25 percent or more being put to death merely because they haven't found anyone who wants them. There is still work to be done: Every year, roughly 4 to 5 million animals are euthanized because they cannot find homes. Like Best Friends Animal Society, more and more nonprofit organizations have sprung up to take in animals and find homes for them. Best Friends aims to be the gold standard: It accepts all kinds of dogs, from the easier-to-adopt, family-friendly pets to the tougher cases, including badly injured dogs and those with a history of undesirable behavior. At Dogtown, all dogs are guaranteed a safe place to live as long as they need it while awaiting placement in a forever home.

Homeless dogs tend to have a few things in common. Many are surrendered when they're between six months and two years old. That corresponds to adolescence and the teenage years in humans and often indicates one of the key reasons why the dogs were given up: Adolescent dogs have passed through the cute puppy phase and have begun to test boundaries, especially if their owners have failed to teach them properly. They may have started habits their human companions disliked, or contributed to frustrations when they appeared resistant to training. Homeless dogs may have passed through difficult times with humans and have suddenly found themselves without a home—and often for no other reason than they acted like normal, healthy dogs who might have responded better had a strong, trusting relationship been in place. These dogs are often perfectly healthy and will make wonderful pets.

Adoption centers of all kinds also often have puppies and older dogs. The former may have been left because their need for constant care overwhelmed their owners. The latter sometimes get dropped off because of medical issues that require intensive supervision, or because their owners have become too old or physically challenged

Adopt. Don't Buy. Best Friends strongly recommends that you adopt a dog instead of buying one from a pet store, online, or the newspaper. Most dogs sold in pet stores are the products of "puppy mills," the inhumane dog-breeding operations despised by true dog lovers. Dogs in puppy mills are forced to have litter after litter while living lives nearly devoid of attention and affection. Mill puppies often are raised on the cheapest food and often have medical problems from malnutrition or being raised in an unsanitary environment. If taken too soon from their mothers, they may be placed in store windows before learning proper social skills. Their purchase, even by well-meaning buyers, keeps cold, hard cash—the lifeblood of puppy mills—flowing into the pockets of unscrupulous breeders. Breeders who truly care about what happens to their dogs will not sell to a pet store, period.

to care for them anymore. These dogs may need special attention and care.

Most adoptable dogs are lovable mixed breeds. Some shelters and groups may have a general idea about the dog's genetic history, but little reliable information about the dog's background may be available in many cases. Rather than focus on the breeding, focus on the aspects you've targeted in your self-assessment sketch. What kind of dog would fit best in your life has more to do with the individual dog's age, size, and energy level. Although a breed history can give you a rough idea of a dog's potential traits and health history, it can't tell you anything definitive. The best thing to do is speak with the dog's caregivers and to meet the dog yourself whenever possible.

Purebred dogs are available through adoption; Petfinder.com, the largest Internet database for homeless pets, reports that at least 25 percent of dogs given up for adoption are purebred. If you're interested in mixed-breed "designer" hybrids (such as a peekapoo—half Pekingese and half poodle—to a buggs—Boston terrier and pug), you can find them through rescue groups and animal shelters as well.

When a dog is surrendered to a shelter or rescue group, she usually goes through some simple tests. Evaluators check the dog's temperament and basic health, including evidence of her having been vaccinated. Staff and volunteers likely will take the time to play with the dog and try to get to know her behavior patterns so they can help make the best match for her. The search for an adoptive home can begin.

Many shelters and rescue groups use foster homes to house dogs while they wait to find their forever homes. Volunteers or staff take the dogs home for a while, working with them to be good companions, until they can be adopted. Many do so with one dog after another, keeping a line of adoptable dogs moving into new homes. Many find themselves deeply moved by the experience.

Dogs placed in foster homes by shelters or rescue groups usually have enough time in a home environment to be themselves, giving the foster family strong insight into the dog's personality, likes and dislikes, and interactions with new people and new situations. A foster family likely knows about a dog's individual temperament, including such things as whether she is housetrained, enjoys playing ball, is good with children or other pets, or requires a lot or a little exercise.

"A foster family is going to have some idea about whether the dog is good with kids, or can be left alone in the house without being destructive," Whitney says. "You'll still need to get to know the dog before you decide to take him home."

Where to Go

When Whitney was in high school, she helped raise guide dog puppies and often spent her afternoons and weekends at a county Humane Society in California, where she worked with 20 to 30 dogs daily. A government-run animal control shelter occupied the same building. Once in a while, if the Humane Society had available room, Whitney went next door, picked out adoptable dogs who likely faced euthanasia, and brought them under the society's wing. Both the animal control shelter and the Humane Society worked to get their dogs into forever homes, but the latter had more time to work with the dogs, learn their behaviors, and try to find them good homes.

Considering all of Whitney's experience, she has seen a wide range of places to adopt a dog and has a short answer when asked where to find the perfect dog.

"The best place is where people really know the dog," she says. Any organization that spends time with its dogs should have some information available to answer questions prospective adopters ask. Those organizations that cannot afford to give much individual attention to the dogs obviously won't know as much. Remember that dogs everywhere deserve loving homes. The most wonderful dog for you could be found almost anywhere you look if you take the time to get to know him.

There are four basic places to begin looking for dogs available for adoption: municipal animal control facilities; nonprofit Humane Societies; locally based rescue groups, including breed-specific rescue groups; and large-scale rescue organizations, such as the American Society for the Prevention of Cruelty to Animals (ASPCA) and Best Friends, which operate beyond the confines of a particular community or region.

In addition to places you can physically visit to check out dogs available for adoption, many virtual sites are available on the Web. The adoption site Petfinder.com works with thousands of rescue organizations and shelters dedicated to finding good homes for pets. It also has good advice about training and caring for dogs and other animals. Its searchable database may be a good way to find a dog from a reputable organization near you.

"Petfinder.com is a wonderful place," Whitney says. "I recommend it all the time. The nice thing about Petfinder is that you've got so many options. You are able to see dogs from many additional places versus just the ones at your local shelter."

When responding to any adoption ads, on or off the Web, that individuals place, you'll want to ask plenty of questions. Ideally, you'll be asked a lot of them as well. A person who genuinely cares for a dog will want to be sure he's going to a good family and will want to know what the dog can expect at his new home. Don't be afraid to ask whether you can contact the dog's veterinarian for information about his health and behavior. It's a good idea to use a contract to protect all parties involved and to know how to return the dog if things don't work out.

Animal Control

You can find many great dogs at your local animal control facilities. These can go by various names such as "animal services" or "animal care and control." Animal control facilities are usually run by a city or county and funded by taxpayer dollars. They're charged with safeguarding public health and safety by accepting unwanted animals, rescuing pets from abuse and neglect, and capturing strays. Dogs taken to crowded animal control facilities may be put down if not claimed by their owners or adopted within a specified period of time. It's an option properly seen as a last resort. If finding a dog who may desperately need adoption in a timely manner appeals to you, investigate your local animal control facility to learn more about its policies and programs for surrendered animals.

Many dogs arrive at animal control with little to no background information about them, so caregivers have to rely on firsthand observations to learn things about them. Constant turnover from dogs coming and going means the staff's time to learn about each dog is limited, and thus they have limited information to give to prospective adopters.

Large, community-based animal control facilities typically have searchable databases on the Internet with pictures and brief biographies of dogs. Some, such as Animal Care & Control of New York City, even have a sign-up service on their websites to request an alert when a particular breed is surrendered or is an unclaimed stray. Just beware: Breeds are not always properly identified, especially when mixed. Dogs labeled as being an Australian shepherd may be an Australian cattle dog or a husky may be a malamute or

Akita. That's why it's helpful to know something about dog breeds, or to bring along someone else who's knowledgeable, when adopting from an animal control facility.

If you see a dog on a facility's website who interests you, take a trip during visiting hours to meet him. Have a supervised introduction with shelter staff to learn more about the dog and see how the two of you might get along. Talk with the caregivers to see what they know about the dog and what their general impressions are. Be sure to ask lots of questions to see how this dog might fit in your household. (For more on your first encounter, see "Meeting a Dog" in this chapter and "Your Own Body Language" in Chapter 2, pages 60-62).

Sometimes the search process can be an emotionally overwhelming experience, so try to take someone with you, such as a friend or a relative who can act as a check on you getting emotionally and perhaps irrationally attached too soon to any one dog. If you know a dog trainer, bring her along. An expert will know what to look for in the dogs' behaviors and health. As Whitney says, your companion might tell you that a dog is indeed adorable, but she might also take the time to remind you about what you're seeking in a dog or to discourage a bad match—such as a dog who has a labeled history of being aggressive toward cats when you're a cat owner.

The possibility of a dog's being euthanized can give the selection process a heightened sense of urgency. Because the time frame to choose a dog may be limited, you could feel an understandable impulse to rush the decision to save a life. A second opinion from a friend can temper this feeling and focus you on choosing the best lifelong match for you.

Once you've met the dog and determined that he's the one for you, you'll begin to move through the adoption process. You will most likely pay an adoption fee, which may help cover the cost of housing and feeding animals in the shelter. You'll likely be required to spay or neuter a dog (if you're not, it's a procedure your dog will need anyway). The cost of surgical sterilization and vaccinations typically is added into the adoption fee. Costs can vary widely; in San Diego County, the adoption fee is $69 for puppies and dogs unless they are five years or older, when the fee drops to $35. In Arlington, Texas, the dog adoption fee is $100, but that includes a city license, sterilization, vaccines, a heartworm test, and the implantation of a microchip to locate the dog should he wander away. Contact your local facility to see what the potential costs are in your neighborhood.

Humane Societies

Locally based, privately funded shelters for companion animals are often called Humane Societies. Humane Society shelters have dogs living on site, often for longer than an animal control facility can house them. The dogs typically live in a kennel environment. As with any shelter, quality depends on its owners and operators. A Humane Society shelter near your home probably has a wide selection of dogs from a variety of backgrounds. Many will have information about their dogs, usually with photographs and background information, available on the Web.

As with animal control facilities, Humane Society shelters get most of their dogs due to a dog's behavioral issues, owners who can no longer care for the animal, or an unplanned litter of puppies. Sometimes the reasons for giving up dogs are heartbreaking: The owner suddenly passed away or had some other extreme medical problem, lost a job and could no longer afford to care for the dog, or had to move to a new home that didn't allow pets.

As with animal control facilities, you'll likely find many breeds, ages, and sizes. That variety provides a good opportunity to interact with several individual dogs and begin to get a feel for how they differ. Employees and volunteers at a Humane Society shelter likely have more time to spend with the dogs to know them as individuals. A beagle puppy may be cute, for example, but someone who has worked or played around a particular pup may know whether he's prone to baying, a common trait of hounds. The staff worker or volunteer also may know whether the dog is shy or friendly, is good with children and cats, and likes to play.

Many Humane Societies, as well as animal control facilities and other private shelters, have meet-and-greet rooms in which potential adopters can get to know dogs. Most shelters let visitors take dogs for a walk or play with the dogs, and some even allow them to take the dog home overnight to see how they fit. Any opportunity to spend extra time with a shelter dog improves the likelihood of making an intelligent adoption decision, so take advantage of these opportunities where they exist.

Whitney urges prospective adopters to ask a lot of questions when adopting. "The more history you can find out ahead of time, the better," she says. To that end, ask where the dog came from. If the dog was a stray, ask how the shelter came to be in physical possession of the dog. If she was surrendered by a previous owner, find out why the owner dropped her off at the shelter.

"Do you know if the dog lived in a house? Or lived in a yard? If she was chained up? Was she a member of the family, living a full life, or merely an outdoor dog who got little contact with the family?" Whitney asks. "If she was an outdoor dog, you may not know whether she was housetrained." If she had limited contact with her family, she may need to be trained to have appropriate social skills.

Giving Back

There are many ways to help homeless dogs in addition to adopting them. One way to is to donate time, money, and supplies to the organizations that care for adoptable dogs. Here are some ways you can give:

Volunteer: Many organizations rely on the dedication of volunteers who perform many tasks including animal care and transportation.

Charitable donations: A financial gift can go a long way to help homeless pets. Some organizations allow you to allocate funds to a specific cause. For instance, at Best Friends, you can sponsor a specific dog or designate that your gift go to Best Friends' Guardian Angel program, which provides care for animals with special needs. Check with your local shelter to see what options exist.

Cleaning supplies: Keeping a kennel clean takes a lot of supplies. Donations of household cleaners, laundry detergents, and towels help keep a shelter sparkling.

Pet supplies: Canned dog food, dog beds, new hard rubber toys (such as Nylabones and Kongs), and dog treats are always high on wish lists. Check to see if your organization has any preferences before purchasing items to donate.

The needs of each organization are different, so check with them to see what items are highest on their wish lists.

If the dog's history is nothing but a blank, ask yourself whether you are willing to commit to adopting the dog without knowing how much time you must invest in training.

Rescue Groups

Best Friends considers a rescue group or organization that utilizes foster homes to be a place with the strongest odds of you finding the best match for your home. Many rescue organizations don't have a central building like animal control facilities or Humane Societies; instead, a network of volunteers agree to work with a group to care for dogs temporarily until they find forever homes. Because adoptable dogs are cared for in real homes, foster families can give detailed information about dogs' personalities, quirks, likes, and dislikes.

Most rescue organizations choose which dogs they accept. Some groups are breed-specific: A quick search of the Internet with the key word *rescue* and a particular kind of dog reveals groups devoted to virtually every breed, from Golden Retriever Rescue of the Rockies to Yankee Chihuahua Rescue and Adoption, "dedicated to the welfare of New England Chihuahuas." Other groups take in all kinds of dogs regardless of breed history; often these groups work with local shelters and animal control facilities. They may take in dogs who otherwise would be euthanized.

Rescue groups, like their dogs, come in all sizes. Some may consist of just a single person who loves to find homes for abandoned dogs. Others are larger, covering whole states, whereas others may be national organizations with branches in virtually every state and that receive some financial support from national breed clubs. Many Web-based sites, including Petfinder.com, have search engines that allow you to find rescue groups by state, city, and breed.

Often, rescue groups will have a presence on the Web and also list dogs that are available for adoption or for fostering. Rescue groups in your community may also host adoption events at local pet stores and other venues where you can go to meet adoptable dogs in person. It's a great opportunity to see a lot of different dogs, see which ones you like (and which ones like you!), and observe how they interact with other people and other dogs; it's also a good time to ask the rescue volunteers lots of questions about their dogs and policies.

When visiting their sites, keep an eye out for signs of a reputable rescue organization. The group's home page should have information about whether it is nonprofit, what its policies are on accepting and placing dogs, and information about adoption fees. Contact information should also be easy to locate.

To be sure you've found a reputable rescue organization, ask for referrals. Talk to others who have adopted dogs from a particular rescue group, or ask professional dog trainers what they know about local groups. Finally, talk with volunteers, especially those who foster dogs. Ask questions about the rescue group, its history, its organization, and its mission. Ask about their adoption policies and what steps you'll need to take to meet and potentially adopt a dog from them.

Adoption policies will vary from group to group. In general, volunteers will work with rescued dogs and usually place information about their availability on a central Web page the rescue group administers. The group may also work with other agencies and personal networks to find good homes. If potential adopters meet a dog at an adoption event, they begin the process by filling out an application. There may be a waiting period before the dog can go home with you; this is to help avoid impulse adoptions. Many groups will also perform a home visit to make sure that the dog will be well placed into a home best suited to her individual needs.

Policies vary from group to group, so check with your rescue group to learn more about their specific procedures.

If as a potential adopter, you see a dog on a group's website, then directly contact the rescue group to set up an appointment to visit a particular dog. Volunteers fostering dogs often have jobs outside the home, which may make it harder for you to get an appointment in a hurry. The trade-off is that once you meet a dog, her family will likely have a rich trove of firsthand, real-time information about the dog.

A formal application procedure, possibly including a home visit, likely is required to ensure that the adoption from a rescue group is a good fit. Don't misconstrue an in-home visit as an unnecessary intrusion. Rescue groups genuinely want to know as much as they can about a possible adoption to satisfy themselves that a dog has a good chance of staying in a forever home, and an on-site visit can tell them what they need to know.

Other groups may have a trial period, during which the dog comes to live with you, and you try each other out. For instance, NorCal Irish Setter Rescue of Northern California requires adopters to undergo an in-home 30-day trial as a probationary period. All of these efforts are to insure that the right pet is placed in the right home for him to make a lifetime match.

Rescue groups rely on donations of time and money. Many have formally filed with the federal government for nonprofit status. Adoption fees cover some or all of the costs of transporting, vaccinating, spaying or neutering, training, and providing care for rescue dogs. For example, Good Shepherd Rescue of North Texas charges $250 for an adult German shepherd adoption, and Great Dane Rescue Inc., based in the Upper Midwest, charges $300. The cost varies from group to group, so be sure to research the costs carefully when considering this option. Adoption fees may seem high, but they are much less expensive than the purchase of a dog.

Lastly, if a rescue group rejects your adoption application, be sure that you understand the reasons. You may be able to make changes in your home or lifestyle that would make a later reapplication successful.

Best Friends Animal Society

Best Friends combines the best elements of Humane Society shelters and rescue groups. It takes in dogs from all over the United States, including some of the most egregious cases of dog abuse, neglect, and abandonment. It has rescued dogs from NFL quarterback Michael Vick's dogfighting operation; from the devastation of Hurricane Katrina and the war-torn Middle East; and from "hoarders," well-intentioned people often with mental illness who take in more animals than they can possibly care for. Best Friends works directly with rescue groups and animal control facilities that have had a difficult time placing a dog. As a first step to help the groups and facilities, Best Friends uses their network to try to place these dogs in homes. If they are unable to find a home after exhausting all other options, and if there is space available, Best Friends sometimes accepts these dogs.

Prospective adopters can drive to Kanab, Utah, or fly into Las Vegas or Salt Lake City (the closest airports to Dogtown) and then drive to meet the dogs living at Best Friends Animal Society. Some people arrive already having dogs in mind from visiting the Best Friends website at www.bestfriends.org. In addition, hundreds of volunteers give their time, often as a vacation, to helping Best Friends. Hours spent in close contact with needy dogs often results in a unique bonding experience.

If you're interested in adopting from Best Friends, you must fill out an application, available on the Web or through an adoption coordinator at the sanctuary. You'll need to provide information about yourself, your home, your plans for training the dog, and so on. You can specify a dog that caught your eye on the Best Friends website, or talk by phone or email with an adoption coordinator who will ask questions to try to make a good match.

If the application is approved, Best Friends will check references for a veterinarian and, if appropriate, a landlord to be sure a rental lease allows a dog. After that, Best Friends arranges for a home check, which a local volunteer often completes. Best Friends has volunteers all over the country who are willing to verify information on an application form and assess the potential for a good adoption.

"We use our network members to do home visits for us," Whitney says. "They will see if there are animals currently in the house, and whether they are cared for. They'll check to see if dogs in the house look happy and healthy, or miserable and skinny."

Best Friends encourages adopters to come to Kanab to meet the dogs, particularly if the one they want to adopt has special needs, but an in-person visit is not absolutely necessary. Best Friends charges an adoption fee of $100 ($125 for puppies), which includes spaying or neutering, vaccinations, microchip implantation, and tests for Lyme disease, heartworm, and ehrlichia. Additional charges apply for dogs that must be shipped by plane.

Best Friends says any reputable rescue organization will require spaying or neutering. Furthermore, Best Friends won't approve an adoption into a home where an existing dog is sexually intact. "It goes against what we do," Whitney says, referring to Best Friends' aim to reduce breeding that contributes to unwanted dogs being abandoned. "If they're not breeding, then why is the dog not fixed? We may say, 'We'll take your application now, but you can't adopt a dog until your current dog is fixed.'" In addition to reducing unwanted litters, spaying and neutering usually has a positive impact on a dog's behavior. Intact males can be harder to train and, in some cases, are more likely to be aggressive.

Dogtown at Best Friends has hundreds of dogs, plenty for anyone who wants to compare before making a decision. Each dog receives an evaluation from Best Friends' veterinary staff and dog training professionals to help learn about the new arrivals. Dogs receive the training they need to help them adjust to sanctuary life or being social, friendly pets. Dogs get good food, plenty of play time, medical care, and one-on-one training from staff and volunteers.

Their stories often touch the hearts of people who visit online or in person. Wilson, a honey-and-white mixed breed, arrived at Dogtown from a dog dealer who planned to sell him to a laboratory for medical experiments. He came to Dogtown after a federal raid shut down the dealer. Now he's a poster boy for Best Friends, looking serenely at the camera on the organization's Web page.

The society works with every dog to try to modify behavioral problems. Sometimes the process takes years. Best Friends doesn't mind; every dog has a home at Dogtown as long as it's needed.

"Basically, everyone here is considered adoptable to the right home," Whitney says.

Meeting a Dog

In most cases before you adopt a dog, you'll be able to meet and get to know each other. These early meetings are important ones for determining if the dog is a good match. Before taking any action, spend as much time as possible just observing the dog as he interacts with the staff and volunteers at the shelter or rescue. Study the dog's body language as he's groomed, handled, and played with. Seeing how he interacts with others might give you a clue as to how he may behave with you.

Meeting a New Dog

1 Turn your body sideways toward the dog. Keep your body relaxed with your hands at your sides. Do not stare directly at the dog's eyes. Wait for him to approach and then sniff you.

2 If the dog comes up to you, pet the dog under his chin with the back of your hand for one second. Do not pet the dog on the top of his head because reaching over him might frighten him. Remove your hand to see if he asks for more petting by moving closer to you.

3 If the dog's body is loose and wiggly, and if his eyes, ears, and mouth are relaxed, then pet the side of his body without leaning over the dog. Withdraw your hand again after a second to "see" what he's telling you. If he asks for more attention, give it to him.

In an initial introduction to a dog you're considering adopting, you can get an idea of any obvious, major issues. Keep in mind that a rescue dog is likely to have been unsettled by the experience of having her family and comfortable home replaced with strange surroundings. So, when you first encounter each other, give her some time to adjust to your presence. Ideally when the dog is ready, let her come to you instead of making a possibly intimidating approach. To make yourself less frightening, bend down on one knee or sit on a stool or chair. The dog may sniff you and look you over. If you feel comfortable, see if the dog is open to being scratched on the side or neck. Ask if you can give the dog a treat, and then see if the dog has been trained to sit and take the treat gently.

Check body language of the entire dog. Look to see if she seems relaxed and happy, or whether she cowers and leans away from you (see Chapter 2). The dog may show signs of anxiety, and that's not unusual. Yawning, panting, lip licking, and other signs of stress may indicate the dog has yet to get comfortable. That's not necessarily bad, as a lot of dogs who are anxious at their first encounter turn out to be great companions. Others stay anxious for a long time, and you may have to work to bring them out of their shells.

Observe the dog's body to assess any potential health or behavioral issues. Does the dog appear healthy? Check the condition of his coat and skin. Ask a staff member to help you physcially assess the dog. Whitney says that when she meets a dog who may be a candidate for living at Best Friends, she does a lot of things a veterinarian or groomer might do. She checks teeth and gums, the dog's feet, back, and rump for sensitivity issues, watching to see if he tries to avoid the touch or snap at the handling. She looks at the whole dog to see how he holds his body, if he is relaxed or uncomfortable, and whether he has any lumps or disfigurements. If the dog has a food bowl or toys, she'll look for obvious signs of guarding behavior, in which the dog might defend his possessions. Potential medical issues can be a concern for any adopters who will need to pay for care. "Lots of medical and behavioral things you can't find out in a brief meeting, but try to find out as much as you can," Whitney says. "Anything to help you make an informed decision."

Ask if you can take the dog for a walk. Check how the dog reacts to being on a leash. Watch to see whether he has any problems with his legs or hips. Pay special attention to how the dog reacts when meeting other people, dogs, and anything else they might encounter. When you return, ask about anything unusual you've noticed.

You might try this with several dogs. Then, go home and think over whether one or more seemed like a good fit. Don't rush into a decision. Plan to return and interact with the dogs again.

If you make repeated visits to a dog up for adoption, compare each visit with the ones before. Does the dog's behavior change? Does he still look happy, with loose and wiggly body language, or is he tense? A dog's behavior may change in various environments or with various people. "A dog may start out perfect, and then after he feels comfortable, some old habits might pop up as his true self or behavior emerges," Whitney says. If that's the case, how long it takes for the dog to become comfortable depends on the dog.

Family Matters

Family needs to take part in the process as well. Take your spouse with you either when you begin the search or when you've narrowed it to a few candidates. Both partners must agree on which dog to adopt, or one may end up regretting the decision and possibly undercutting the dog's training. Self-assessments, as discussed in Chapter 1, are best done by the adults in a family. Children's input should be welcome, but the decision should rest with parents.

Best Friends recommends that your whole family meet a dog once you're strongly considering a few candidates for adoption before bringing one home. A meeting away from home may not always be possible, but it's the ideal way to see how the dog behaves with everyone you want to share her life. You'll soon know whether the dog blends easily with your family, or if you see behaviors you want to work on. Keep in mind you won't get a complete picture of how the dog will react to your home until she has been there awhile.

Once you have found a dog that you think will be a good fit for your family, then you will want to let your children meet her. Be sure to evaluate the dog's body language as she interacts with your children—or better yet, have a trainer on hand to offer an expert's opinion.

If other dogs are in your household, you should try to arrange an introduction before you bring your adoptee home. Staff members from where you're adopting should be able to help set up a supervised introduction on neutral territory to see how the dogs might interact. Having an experienced staff member or dog trainer on hand will be key to measuring how well the introduction goes. If it does not go well, they can provide the insight you'll need about your adoption decision.

This first meeting could be in a shelter's visiting room or in a neutral location such as a dog park, a neighbor's yard, or a friend's house. Best Friends recommends that both dogs should be on leashes with calm adult handlers. The dogs should be kept at a safe distance and walked side by side. Next, the handlers should cross paths and allow the dogs to smell where the other dog has been. If all is going well to this point, then the dogs can meet (see Chapter 8 for more on dog introductions). If the dogs are comfortable, they will sniff each other and perhaps engage in some play behavior. If they are uncomfortable, one or both may display signs of fear, anxiety, or even aggression (see Chapter 2 for more on body language and mood). Some dogs may take repeated introductions to warm up to each other. If the introductions make you unsure of how this new dog may fit into your home, talk about your concerns with the shelter staff or an experienced dog trainer to see what might be possible.

Although an initial interaction may go well, Best Friends recommends giving dogs a chance to get to know each other under supervision as behaviors can change over time. Special caution should be taken when leaving a new dog with cats, smaller dogs, or any animal who is significantly smaller or bigger than the new pet.

Plan for Success

Although stories of successful adoption through love at first sight make the rounds at Dogtown, they tend to be the exception and not the rule. Whitney cautions against choosing a dog by impulse. Remember why you want a dog and what the best fit will be for your home and lifestyle, as described in Chapter 1. Take your time to pick the right dog. The hard work of your self-assessment and successful navigation of the adoption process will pay off with stronger chances for a great relationship with your new dog.

Top Tips

•Wonderful adoptable dogs can be found at animal control facilities, privately funded animal shelters, rescue groups (both local and nationwide), and reputable online resources, like Petfinder.com.

•Almost any kind of dog—purebred or mutt, big or small, young or old—can be found. Use the sketch from your self-assessment to help guide your search.

•When visiting adoption venues, it's a good idea to bring along a friend or a dog trainer (if you know one) to help you find the best match for you and your lifestyle.

•Ask the dog's caregivers a lot of questions about his history, potential medical issues, behavior, and personality. Learn everything you can about the dog before you proceed with an adoption.

•When first meeting a potential adoptee, don't rush the introduction. Allow the dog some time to adjust to your presence and then let her approach and sniff you. If her body is relaxed and loose, try petting her briefly under the chin to see if she's receptive.

Bringing your dog home is exciting for both you and your new best friend.
Be sure to have his "pad" all ready to go before the big day arrives.

Be Prepared

You've got a lot to do before you bring your dog home. There's the practical: buying food and toys and picking out a vet. There's the logistical: preparing your house for a newcomer who can be as curious and vulnerable as a baby. And then there's the procedural: You and the rest of your family need to agree on the rules of the house and how to enforce them. Dogs appreciate not only knowing they have a safe and welcoming environment, but also what's expected of them as members of the household. So, be prepared to teach them how to act.

House Rules

It's a commonly made mistake—we bring a new dog into our homes and just expect him to know what to do. But a dog needs to have the rules taught to him and consistently reinforced, so before the dog arrives, figure out what the house rules are going to be. Rules should include whether the dog will have access to the entire home, or just to a limited number of rooms. You'll also want to decide whether the dog is allowed on the couch or bed. Once you make up your mind, stick with the rules; don't confuse the dog and invite behavior you don't want or may not want in the future. The idea is to give the dog a framework to shape his behavior, instead of giving him free rein and then having to deal with resulting problems.

If you give your dog the run of the house, keep in mind that it is easier for her to get into things you'd rather she not have access to. She may wander off to relieve herself in another room, or dig into the shoes in your closet until she finds just the right ones to chew. Until your dog has been housetrained, you should consider limiting her movements so you can keep an eye on her all the time. Best Friends dog trainer Whitney Jones recommends putting baby gates in your doorways. They are cheap and easy to install, and quickly allow you to open or close a room to a dog while allowing adults and cats through. Installing gates outside a bedroom where the dog sleeps or at the entrance to the kitchen will limit nighttime wandering and mischief. Try making carpeted rooms off-limits at first so any accidents will be easy to clean.

If you don't want to buy and install baby gates, or gates don't conform to your floor plan, consider alternatives for times when you can't directly supervise her movement. You could clip a four- to six-foot lead to your pants with a carabiner while working in the kitchen or office, for example, or tie her leash to something immobile while you work nearby. Another alternative, described in detail later in this chapter, is crate training your dog.

As for furniture, there's nothing inherently wrong with letting your dog sleep on a bed or a couch. However, you may have reasons to keep her off. She is almost certain to shed, which may require daily cleanings. She may drool, leaving wet spots where you normally would sit. She may take up a lot of room on your bed. If you sleep alone, having a dog in bed with you probably won't matter very much. If you share a bed, or someday plan to do so, it might be easier to train the dog to stay on the floor from the beginning.

"My dogs can be on the couch but not on the bed," says dog trainer Ann Allums. "They have doggie beds that are very comfortable, and I started them using the doggie beds on Day One. If you start with a dog on the bed, it's a little harder to change the rules after that." But if you start a dog sleeping on the floor, you should have little trouble getting the dog in bed with you later, should you change your mind.

Ann has one other bedside rule: She does not like her dogs to paw her awake in the morning. She ignores them until she wants to get up. Even if it's time to get out of bed, she doesn't want them to think that pawing her will bring results, so she waits until the dogs have been quiet for a few minutes before arising. Ann has also instituted this rule from Day One, and it will pay dividends on weekends when you want to sleep late. If you don't allow your dog to wake you, you'll need to observe her to figure out her morning routine. Many pawings and whimperings can be safely ignored; others may indicate the dog really needs to relieve herself.

Other rules to be decided in advance:

- How often will you walk and play with your dog?
- Will you allow your dog to beg for treats from your dinner table?
- Where will the dog sleep?
- Will you let your dog jump on you or other people?
- Will you allow your dog unsupervised access to the kitchen, laundry room, or bathroom?

•Will you let your dog bring in toys, bones, and other objects from outdoors? They may be OK on the linoleum of a kitchen floor but leave stains on a carpet.

Whatever you decide, continue reinforcing those rules to minimize undesirable behavior (see Chapter 7).

Dogproof Your Home

Parents of toddlers learn to look at their homes from a small child's point of view: The perspective of sitting on the floor and looking around the house opens up a whole new world. Potential danger spots—such as electrical sockets, household cleaners on the floor of the pantry or below the sink, and the choking hazard of curtain ropes—become more apparent.

You'll learn much the same if you try to see your house from your dog's point of view. Get down on the floor and check out what your dog might see and smell. Look for exposed wooden table and chair legs. They may make tempting chew targets for dogs, especially teething puppies. You may find how easy it is to get into the shoes in the closet if the door is left open. Your dog certainly may, too, so you will want to remove the temptation for turning your footwear collection into a pile of chew toys. Beware of giving your dog an old shoe as a toy. A dog won't differentiate between "toy" shoes and the nice ones you wear, so it's best not to give shoes at all (see Chapter 7 for more on chewing).

Try to put any children's toys, especially the plush kind, beyond the dog's reach. This may require training the children too. A child's failure to put a toy back in a box or on a high shelf may lead to its destruction. Although that could be a good lesson to the child in the long run, it's not a good habit for the dog to begin.

Food is always a great temptation for dogs, so take a look at your pantry and kitchen cupboards to see what "treats" he might discover. You also may find cabinet doors that open with just a nudge to reveal bread, crackers, and other food. Simple baby locks that open with the push of a finger will defeat many persistent dogs. Others are strong enough to force such locks, and for them, you probably will want to raise food items high above their access.

Look for poisonous plants in your house. Remove them from anywhere the dog can chew on them. The best way to learn if your plants contain toxins is to look them up on the Web. Common house and yard plants that are harmful to dogs include dieffen-bachia, tomato plants, oleander, yucca, aloe vera, yew, American bittersweet, English ivy, mistletoe, morning glory, and a wide variety of flower bulbs including daffodil, day lily, gladiolus, hyacinth, iris, narcissus, and tulip. Don't think a potential problem has been solved by moving a plant to a table or bookshelf. Poisonous leaves may fall to the floor, or the plant may get knocked over.

Yard Rules

If you intend to let your dog into a fenced yard, check the fence's height and integrity. A four-foot-high fence may be enough for some dogs, but others may be able to escape by jumping or climbing. You may need a higher fence. Stockade-style fences, which stand about six feet high, should be sufficient to keep most dogs inside, but be sure you don't have a bench or table next to the pickets that your dog could use as a launch pad.

Examine the base by walking the entire fence line. Look for holes where the dog could crawl under, or soft spots where she could dig her way out. Best Friends prevents dogs tunneling out of their runs by burying the bottom of its fences. If your fence already is in place and doesn't have a secure bottom edge, consider lining it with rocks or attaching a skirt of chicken wire and burying it under a light layer of dirt, leaves, and other debris to discourage digging.

Many dogs enjoy time outside, but make sure you've got enough playthings to keep him entertained. A dog alone in an empty yard will find ways to entertain himself, which can lead to destructive behavior. Have some toys available in the yard to keep your dog occupied. You also might consider making a few changes to your backyard to stimulate your dog's body and mind. Dogs like to dig, a fact you can use to your advantage by installing a sand pit and encouraging your dog to excavate there instead of in your grass. Burying things in the sand for your dog to discover can be fun (see Chapter 7 for more on digging).

You may want to confine your dog to certain parts of the yard, away from flowerbeds, vegetable gardens, or new sod. In particular, make sure your dog cannot get into any poisonous plants. You could install a short barrier, such as landscaping timbers or a more

Clean Up. While out for a walk, your dog may relieve herself along the way. Be sure to clean up any "presents" she may leave behind. Many dog owners prefer the convenience of small plastic bags to pick up messes without dirtying their hands. It's easy: Insert your hand inside a bag and turn it inside out so it covers your palm and fingers like a sock. Reach down to pick up the poop. With your free hand, grab the top edge of the bag and pull away from your body to turn it inside out again, with the poop inside. Tie off the top of the bag and discard it in your trash bin. Biodegradable bags are available for purchase on the Web and at some pet stores.

formal fence. Or you could use the power of rewards to shape your dog's behavior so she wants to venture only into certain parts of the yard. Getting your dog to go potty in just one part of the yard simplifies cleanup and helps keep kids out of unpleasant messes (see Chapter 5 for discussion of strategic use of rewards to shape behavior in desired patterns). Finally, you may want to buy a poop scooper and a rake to clean up your yard. Cheap and easy to use, they simplify cleanup.

Best Friends doesn't recommend installing electronic fences, which operate by sending a shock from the buried perimeter to a receiver in a dog's collar. The receiver creates an unpleasant sensation as the dog approaches the perimeter. Electronic fences have two drawbacks. First, any dog who has enough motivation will ignore the irritation and charge through the fence line. Second, such fences do nothing to prevent outside animals, who aren't wearing specialized collars, from entering your yard and harming your dog.

Every dog with a yard deserves a place to get out of the sun (or any other weather) when he is playing outside. A small shelter or store-bought doghouse provides a secure, dry, and shaded place with added protection from the elements.

Comfort Food

The transition of bringing a dog into your home can involve some stress for your new dog, as well as for you. One thing that can help reduce your new dog's stress level is keeping his food consistent with his routine. If possible, find out what your new dog has been eating, along with how much and how often he was being fed. Keep this routine in place when he comes home to live with you. The familiar tastes, smells, and feeding times will be a comfort to him.

If you wish to change his food, make sure to change slowly as new foods can sometimes cause your dog digestive problems that could include diarrhea, intestinal gas, or other unpleasant physical symptoms. A standard for switching a dog's food is the "20 percent rule." Start by adding 20 percent of the new food, to 80 percent of the old food for a day or two. Watch your dog's stools, and if they remain firm, then proceed to mixing 40 percent of the new food to 60 percent of the old food for a couple of more days until you end up giving 80 percent of the new food and 20 percent of the old food.

You should serve your dog's meal in stainless steel or ceramic bowls. The surface of plastic bowls is so porous they are almost impossible to get completely clean. In addition, dogs who eat out of plastic bowls may get skin irritations that look like acne. Another advantage of using stainless steel or ceramic dog dishes is that most dogs cannot chew on them.

What to Eat: Best Friends recommends feeding your dog a high-quality food that is appropriate for your dog's activity level. Assessing the quality of a dog food can be tricky, unless you know what to look for in the ingredient list. Try not to let fancy packaging or flashy commercials influence your dog food decision. Instead, try to educate yourself and use the following as guidelines when reading a dog food label. Dog food labels list the contents in decreasing percentage of composition, meaning the most common ingredients appear first on the list.

If you look at a dog's teeth, you will see that his teeth are sharp, designed to tear meat off bones, rather than flat to grind grains. Dogs are meat eaters, and for this reason, you will want to select a food that has one or two named animal protein sources in the first five ingredients. In addition to identifiable animal proteins, you'll also want to look for a food that contains whole vegetables, fruits, and grains, such as brown rice. Avoid any food with corn or wheat at the top of the list, as foods containing high amounts of these grains can often cause allergies and may not provide adequate nutrition. Whitney says she has seen reactions including itchiness, red and rough skin rashes known as "hot spots," ear infections, and hair loss in dogs who are fed a low-quality diet or who have existing allergies.

When reading a dog food label, avoid foods that contain added sweeteners or artificial colors. You'll also want to avoid artificial preservatives, such as butylated hydroxyanisole (BHA), butylated hydroxytoluene (BHT), and ethoxyquin. Instead, look for a food that is kept fresh with a natural preservative, such as tocopherols (forms of vitamin E), vitamin C, or rosemary extract. Keep in mind that feeding your dog a high-quality food can end up saving you money by keeping your dog healthier and helping you avoid expensive veterinary bills.

Healthy Weight: Just as with people, not all dogs metabolize their food at the same rate. Metabolism of food can be based on heredity, activity level, or age, so know your dog and try to balance the amount of calories she takes in with the amount of calories she burns off. "There are so many different versions of foods out there," Whitney says. "If you have a really active dog, you may want something geared toward a more active dog. As opposed to, say, a senior formula, which is geared toward a dog that is typically less active." Don't assume a young dog automatically needs to ingest more calories than a mature or elderly dog. As Best Friends often says, it depends on the dog.

When your new dog first arrives home, you'll want to note her weight and get a veterinarian's opinion about what your dog's ideal weight should be. Once you know where your dog's current weight is

Continues on p. 102

Body Condition

Keeping your dog at a healthy weight is an important part of his healthcare regimen. Being too fat or too thin can cause serious health problems for your pet. The Texas A&M University "Body Condition Score" rates a dog on a scale from 1 to 5, from emaciated to obese. The perfect score is a 3. To judge your dog's score, look down at the back, ribs, and waistline of your standing dog, and also check the chest and belly in profile.

TOO THIN:

❶ Emaciated: All bony structures (ribs, spine, hips) are prominent. Muscle mass is decreased, and the dog has no fat. The dog's shape has a severe, hourglass-like tuck from above and a dramatic tuck when looking at the abdomen from the side.

❷ Thin: Ribs, lumbar vertebrae, and pelvic bones can be easily seen. The base of the tail appears bony, but has a little soft tissue. The dog has a marked hourglass shape to the waist, but not so severe as to appear emaciated.

IDEAL WEIGHT:

❸ Optimal: Bony structures are easily felt, with a slight cover of fat. The waist has a smooth hourglass shape when seen from above, and a concave abdominal tuck in profile. The base of the tail is smooth with a thin cover of soft tissue.

TOO HEAVY:

4 Fat: The ribs and lumbar vertebrae are harder to feel. The base of the tail is covered with a fat deposit. Seen from above, the dog has no hourglass shape; from the side, she has no tuck where her belly diverges from her rib cage.

5 Obese: The ribs and lumbar vertebrae are very difficult or impossible to feel. Seen from above, the dog's body has a football shape, broad in the middle where a healthy dog would have a slight concavity behind the ribs. The dog's back is markedly broadened. From the side, her belly has no tuck at all, in fact, it may bulge outward.

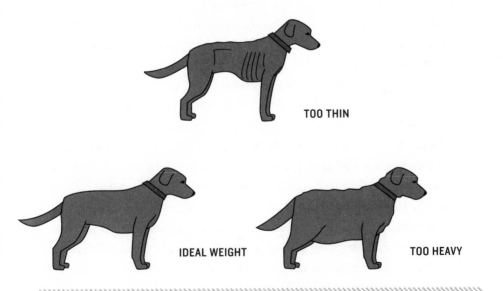

TOO THIN

IDEAL WEIGHT

TOO HEAVY

in relation to her ideal weight, you can select a dog food and a daily amount of that food that would be appropriate for your dog. Often a chart on the back of the bags recommends the serving of food for a dog's age and weight. This can be a good place to start, but be sure to monitor your dog's eating and exercise habits to assess if the amount is right for her. "Most of us agree, you don't want an overweight dog," Whitney says. "Our dogs at Best Friends are very active here. But sometimes people take them home, and *wooo!* They think food equals love, and they overfeed them. It's important to know that too much food is not good for your dog. Keep them at a good weight."

Feeding Time: The next decision you'll have to make for your new dog is how often to feed him. You'll need to take into account not only what seems best for your dog, but also what best fits your schedule and lifetstyle. You may find that your dog only wants to eat once a day, but twice a day may work better with your dog's cycles of sleeping and exercising. "My dogs would like to eat twice a day," Whitney says, "but I don't do mornings, so they eat once a day." Another option is to stretch out your dog's daily ration by giving part of it as a meal and the rest as rewards for good behavior and successful training. Some dogs, including young puppies, usually need to eat more often throughout the day than older dogs, so be sure to consult with your veterinarian when feeding a puppy or young dog.

From a dog-training standpoint, it is best to give your dog scheduled meals, rather than free-feeding (leaving food in the bowl all the time). Scheduled meals can help you develop a better relationship with your dog. In addition, allowing some dogs to eat as much as they want is an invitation to disaster. Some dogs are so highly motivated by food that they eat until it's not good for them. Whitney says, "Once again, it's important to know your dog when deciding how much to feed."

Best Friends has many dogs who need to constantly be kept busy to avoid having them develop behavior issues. In the case of these dogs, sometimes the caregivers can use food and the act of eating as mental stimulation. "We have a lot of dogs here who have a lot of energy, and they need to burn it off," Whitney says. "No matter how much exercise you give them, they need something to do, and so we might transition them from eating from a bowl, to eating out of a food toy, where they have to work to get their food out. If a dog eats really fast, and gorges his food, you might give him food in a toy to slow him down, which will also mentally stimulate him."

Treats and Toys

Have a cache of treats ready before you bring home your dog so you can begin training immediately. The best kind of treat will depend on the dog's preferences. Some dogs will work for kibble, whereas others are motivated by something more "high-value." In case you have a dog with such discriminating taste, you'll want to have a supply of soft, stinky, high-protein treats, such as chicken, cheese, hot dogs, or commercially processed nibbles. Dogs have such a strong sense of smell that they may work harder for a small, smelly treat than a larger, blander one. Remember to take the calories of treats into account.

Some dogs may prefer a toy as a reward instead of a treat or food. You'll want to have some dog toys ready for your new dog to keep his mind and body fit. When you bring your dog home, be prepared to have something the dog can chew or fetch. Chewing is a natural behavior for dogs, so it's good to give them something safe to gnaw, such as a Kong or Nylabone, hard toys not designed to be ingested. Squeaky toys may be right for your dog, or they may get destroyed 30 seconds after dog and toy come together. The bottom line: Offer a variety of toys to get to know your dog's preferences. Puppies need age-appropriate toys. They need to chew as their teeth develop. Kong and other manufacturers make soft versions of toys for dogs who prefer them.

It may take a while for your dog to warm up to treats and toys, especially if she has not been properly socialized. Best Friends trainers found that some dogs rescued from Michael Vick's dogfighting operation lacked understanding of toys and treats. They had existed in a small circle of training, fighting, and confinement in pens. Many did not get a lot of healthy interaction with people or other dogs. "So, when we introduced toys and treats to them, some of them went, 'Woohoo! This is fun!'" Whitney says. "And some of

///

Food Toys You don't have to feed a dog out of a bowl; you can turn your dog's feeding time into a game or lesson by stuffing a toy with food so he has to work to get it out. Best Friends fashions feeding toys out of plain, foot-long sections of PVC pipe, capped at the ends and with holes drilled in the sides to let kibble pass through. Some trainers also use a variety of commercial toys that can be stuffed with food. These include Buster Cubes, Premier Busy Buddy Tug-a-Jug, and Kong Wobbler. All dispense kibble when the dog figures out how she must roll, pull, or tip the toy. Some of the most elaborate require both supervision by and interaction with you. Those manufactured by Nina Ottosson, a Swedish company, require a dog to find food by lifting blocks, moving discs, or pushing buttons. To work the company's "Dog Brick," for example, a dog must remove toy bones and then push aside sliding covers to reveal the treats hidden inside.

them went, 'I don't know what this is.' For them, we had to keep introducing the treats and toys, and teach them how to play. And a lot of them ended up learning to enjoy toys."

Oscar was one of Vick's dogs who took a while to catch on, says Michelle Besmehn, co-manager of dog care at Dogtown. "One of the first times we gave him a treat, he walked up to it, nudged it, and jumped back," she says. "Then he started playing with it. He didn't know what a treat was. Others picked it up much quicker."

Collar and Leash

Buy a flat collar with a buckle or a quick release clasp. It should rest snugly against the dog's neck. Dog owners often leave the collar too loose, allowing the dog to pull free. The proper fit allows you to insert two fingers comfortably between the collar and the neck. The collar should have your dog's ID tags on it with her name and a contact number so that she can be traced back to you if she gets loose.

Attach the collar to a leash. The leash's length is up to you. Six feet is average, and most dog walkers prefer it. If you want to keep your dog closer to you, especially during initial training, a four-foot leash may work better. You might also have a second, longer lead to use in practicing the "come" cue, as explained in Chapter 5 (see pages 138-142).

If the dog tends to pull, you can use a few different kinds of positive training tools to help you manage this behavior. These tools work on the principle that dogs respond to pressure with pressure. For example, have you noticed that if you try to push your dog away, he pushes back into you? The same principle applies if you have a dog who pulls while walking on leash; if you're using a collar or standard harness attached to a leash, a pulling dog puts pressure on his neck or chest, causing him to move into the pressure, resulting in the dog pulling away from you.

The following training tools work by applying gentle pressure to different parts of the dog's body to discourage him from pulling. Head collars, like the Gentle Leader or the Halti, fit over the dog's snout and high on the dog's neck. You might consider a front-clip harness such as Premier's Easy Walk Harness. Another non-pull harness is the Sporn-brand harness, which fits snuggly under the dog's front legs and around the chest. These tools don't necessarily teach a dog not to pull—that's a training exercise you should do using red light–green light techniques outlined in Chapter 5 (see pages 142-144). Instead, alternative halters and harnesses prevent dogs from practicing bad habits and make walking more enjoyable for you.

Places to Rest

It's good advice to let sleeping dogs lie, but they will need a place for that snooze. Some dogs prefer a dog bed. If yours does, try to find one with a removable outer cover that can easily be washed. Beds come in many sizes and shapes, and the right size may not seem to match your dog's body. Some small dogs like to sprawl in big beds, and some big dogs contort themselves into small beds. If your dog chews a lot, you might opt for a Kuranda bed, which looks like a low-slung, cloth-covered end table or a cot. The bed elevates the dog off the floor and its hard plastic shell resists destructive chewing. Older dogs with joint problems might prefer an orthopedic bed containing special foam.

Many dogs like to sleep in dog crates, available at most pet supply stores. Best Friends trainers know crates not only simplify housetraining, as described in Chapter 5, but also provide a dog with a sense of security. In general, the crate should be big enough so that the dog can comfortably stand up, turn around, and lay flat on his side. If you are housetraining your dog, it shouldn't be so large that the dog has room to go potty at one end and sleep at the other; for a housetrained dog, the crate can be as big a you'd like. If your dog is a puppy, buy a larger crate and use a divider to adjust it as he gets bigger.

Experts have found that dogs typically enjoy having their own quiet space where they can feel safe and take breaks from the noise and bustle of a household if they feel the need. "If you set it up right, so a crate is seen as a positive thing, then some dogs really like it," Whitney says.

Trainers at Dogtown keep crates in their offices with the doors propped open. That's where you're most likely to find calm and happy dogs while the trainers work at their desks. The protected, cavelike space often appeals to something primal in the dog, especially if it's oriented so the dog can see the entire room. If a dog prefers to take a break in a quiet place, however, a more isolated location for the crate may be preferred.

Michelle says, "Barnum, one of my beagles in the past, used to lie in the bottom shelf of my bookshelf, which didn't have anything in it, because it was very denlike. He felt safe in there, and it was a quiet place. So a crate can be a great tool for housetraining, but it also can be a nice, quiet safe spot for the dog to get away from the activities of the house when he wants to."

Some dog owners view crating as a punishment. Best Friends dog trainer Jen Severud recalls a conversation with just such a person whose dog had taken out three sets of blinds and three sets of curtains and was chewing inappropriate items. One solution that Jen offered was to teach the dog that being in the crate could be a fun experience and shouldn't be used as punishment. Jen said to her, "You're describing to me a dog who could benefit from a crate because he is wreaking havoc on your home and could actually hurt himself by eating the wrong thing."

A dog should be introduced to a crate slowly and with rewards (see Chapter 5 for how to use during housetraining). A dog thrown into a crate for the first time and left alone for many hours will not like the experience. If properly introduced to a crate, however, the dog likely will choose it as his favorite spot in the house.

To get your dog used to the crate, begin by associating it with good things. Put treats and toys that your dog likes in the crate. If she shows reluctance to enter, place the treats in the crate near the entrance and let her poke her head in to get them. As she grows more comfortable, start placing the treats farther and farther in the crate until she can enter it all the way. Getting your dog acquainted with the crate can take a few hours—or a few days. Just be patient, and don't force her. Teach the dog that the crate is a happy place, and one that you want her to love.

Don't crate an adult dog for more than four hours at a time. If you plan to leave your dog in a crate while you are at work, arrange with someone to visit your house over lunch to let the dog out for a walk and a potty break. Puppies must be let our far more often (a general rule is that puppies can hold their bladders for the number of hours that equals their age in months, plus one). As a rule, the dog should only be spending long periods of time in the crate at night if that's where she will be sleeping.

Looking Good

To keep your dog in tip-top shape, you'll need proper grooming tools. You will want to buy a nail trimmer to help keep your dog's nails at an appropriate length, too. If they get too long, they can cause pain and possible disfigurement. Because the quick grows out with the length of the nail, you have to gradually reduce the size of the nail by gradually taking off the tip over several weeks. This gives the quick time to retract so that you can get the nails back to an appropriate length. Be careful of clipping too much and slicing open a blood vessel. Much like if you tear a fingernail, that causes pain and creates a bad experience that the dog won't want to repeat.

Choose a style of clippers that works best for you. Many dog owners prefer clippers that look like scissors, which can be carefully positioned before trimming the end of the nail. Others prefer a guillotine-style clipper. You may want to purchase a styptic pencil

Shopping List
Before you bring your dog home, there's a lot of gear you're going to need. Here's a quick shopping list for your new best friend:

- Dog crate
- Dog bed
- Food dish
- Water bowl
- Dog food
- Training treats
- Various types of toys
- Hairbrush and/or comb

- Flat collar with a buckle or clasp and leash
- Nail clippers and styptic pencil or quick blood stopper
- Enzyme-based dog odor remover for house-training mishaps
- Optional: baby gates, dog shampoo

or a powder that will stop bleeding quickly for any cuts you accidentally inflict, although ordinary flour may work in a pinch.

For grooming, choose brushes to match your dog's coat. You may want soft bristles and a comb for shorter hair, and something longer and stiffer for wire- or long-haired dogs. You might have to brush a long-haired dog daily to keep her coat from matting. The more you brush, the more the dog's loose hairs pull free and the less likely she is to shed. Most dogs find a good brushing to be relaxing. If your dog objects to being brushed, you can work on changing the dog's behavior by associating brushing with good things such as treats.

You may want to clean your dog's teeth yourself with a specially formulated dog toothbrush and toothpaste, instead of leaving basic dental care to a vet. If you want to brush your dog's teeth, begin slowly to let the dog get used to the idea. Regular brushing will help prevent the buildup of plaque, which requires a professional cleaning.

Find Pet Professionals

Finding great providers of medical care and grooming is essential before bringing your dog home. If you don't already have a veterinarian whom you trust, get a recommendation from a friend with dogs, or from a trusted trainer. Then go to the veterinarian's office without your dog. Give the building, employees, and dog clients your complete attention, and watch for things that might signal potential problems. Look to see if the lobby is clean, or if it smells like urine. Check to see if the staff is friendly. Ask to see where dogs are boarded if the vet has a kennel in which you may be considering boarding your dog. Look for signs of competence, high-quality care, and genuine love of animals.

You might consider meeting the veterinarian just to talk, or to introduce him or her to your dog before your pet actually needs medical care. Observe how the vet interacts with your dog and with other clients. Is the vet calming and comforting? How does the dog react? You'll want a veterinarian who is patient, particularly if you have adopted a rescue dog. As you won't know much, if any, of the history of an adopted dog, it's possible your dog has had a bad experience with a veterinarian. If your dog appears uncomfortable, you'll need patience while you are helping your dog to get used to the vet.

Finally, trust your instincts. "If your gut says you don't feel comfortable with this person, leave," Whitney says. "Find somebody else."

Follow a similar process when choosing a groomer. You probably will want to stay with your dog the first time she is groomed so you can watch how the groomer handles her and how she responds. Keep in mind, however, that some dogs behave worse when their owner is present—and if that's the case, leave.

Some groomers may let you watch as they groom other dogs, perhaps in a shop window. Check to see how they restrain the dog. Many dogs resist being clipped or brushed and need to be held in place. It is important to pick a groomer who has a gentle, patient demeanor and who will not handle the dog aggressively. A good groomer loves working with animals—even the challenging ones.

Homecoming

When you first bring home your dog, remember you are helping him adjust to an entirely different world. Take things slowly to reduce anxiety. Introduce her to only part of the house at first, and gradually allow her more and more access. Pay close attention to your dog's behavior for the first few weeks as she passes through this "honeymoon" period in your relationship. The actions you see at first may not last. As your dog's confidence rises, her behavior may get better—or worse. Plan to include all family members in play, exercise, cleanup, training, and other activities involving the dog. This will help your new addition bond with everyone in the house.

If you have a cat, let your new dog gradually get adjusted to the second pet. Allow your dog to smell the cat's presence in the house before you introduce them, leaving the cat in a safe part of the house. Make the introduction slowly. Your cat should always have a place to get away from your dog, whether it is access to a high shelf or another room where the dog cannot go. Your new dog should never be left alone with the cat for any length of time: There is always an element of risk in leaving dogs and cats unattended together. Even if they have gotten along for years, unanticipated events can change their interaction. Play can escalate, illness can change behavior, or an outside stimulus can trigger a negative interaction.

It is important for your new dog to have exposure to new people but this should be done gradually. Don't overwhelm an already stressed dog by throwing a loud, confusing party to welcome him home the very first day. Some dogs might welcome a stream of introductions, but others may feel overwhelmed and protect themselves by hiding from human contact. Pay attention to your dog's reactions in the new home and try to make him feel more comfortable. Unusual things that seem harmless to humans, such as ceiling fans, may cause fear in a dog who hasn't seen them before.

Your new dog may be stressed when she spends the first night in your home. It's bound to tug at your heartstrings. Once you've ruled out any other cause for the dog's distress (Is she thirsty? Does she need to relieve herself?), just be confident that your patience will help the new dog settle in. If you plan on using a crate, keep it close enough to where you sleep so that you can hear and respond to any signs of distress. Puppies may whimper and bark because they need to go potty, which they will need to do about one to two times during the night, depending on their age. An older dog may also need to eliminate during the nighttime hours and will most likely try to alert you if he needs to go out.

When your dog finally settles into his new home and his anxiety abates, it's time to focus on her training. Every interaction between you and your dog is an opportunity for learning, from the first moment she comes home. By making sure your house is set up properly, establishing a set of commonly shared house rules, and having the proper doggie equipment on hand, you're bound to get off to a great start.

Top Tips

•Before your dog comes home, establish the house rules and stick to them. Make sure everyone in the house abides by them.

•Know what rooms you want your dog to have access to and where you'd like her to sleep at night.

•Dogproof your house and yard to keep everyone safe. Remove hazardous things (such as poisonous plants, chocolate, and lit candles). Place precious things and keepsakes out of your dog's reach.

•Have the proper food and plenty of treats on hand when you bring your dog home.

•When looking for a new vet or groomer, pay attention to the building and staff. Is the facility clean and well kept? Do the staff radiate confidence, competence, and a commitment to high-quality care? Do you sense a genuine love of animals?

Sherry Woodard rewards Sophie with tasty treats and praise. Figuring out what motivates your dog will improve your training sessions.

5

Relationship-Based Training

Lila, a black-and-white American pit bull terrier, paces just inside the fence. She's new to Dogtown, and she's nervous. She clacks her jaw and fixes a laserlike gaze on the people outside her pen.

Who knows what Lila thinks as she looks at the newcomers? Before coming to Dogtown, she was part of a dogfighting operation in Missouri. Nobody is certain whether she fought in a ring, served as a "bait dog" to provoke fighting among dogs in training, or simply cranked out puppies to refresh the owner's fighting stock. But there are clues. She's had at least one litter. And the lines on her face, where gray hairs have grown to cover a cobweb-like network of scars, bear mute testimony to a violent past. For all she knows, strangers may bring more violence. Lila has reason to be nervous.

"She needs some time to adjust to being here," says Ann Allums, a certified professional dog trainer at Best Friends. "Today, we're just going to work on not being afraid."

That may mean starting some simple training through the fence, with Ann on one side and Lila on the other, where she can move away if she feels uncomfortable. Ann might start by walking along the fence, giving a treat every time she passes Lila. The dog might then begin to associate humans with good things. Maybe Ann will give rewards in return for Lila exhibiting some basic movements, which over time could be shaped into a more specific action, such as a "Down," or some other behavior. Getting complex behavior from Lila is in the future though. On this day, Ann and the other trainers will be content merely to start at the very beginning, by building a trusting relationship.

Learning From the Start

No matter if your dog has a traumatic past or is just a newborn pup, all dogs begin their relationship with you from the first moment you meet. Dogs, like children, are information-gathering machines. They constantly observe what others do. They live in the moment, testing various behaviors to see what happens. It's vital to be ready to teach the right things from the very first meeting. It's never too early to start good training habits.

Some trainers at Best Friends love working with puppies because younger dogs likely don't have bad habits to unlearn or long-held fears to overcome. "Trainers get excited when we have puppies, because the puppies' brains are like little sponges," says trainer Jen Severud, who ran her own dog-training business in Minnesota before coming to Best Friends in 2008. "You can teach them anything." Optimal learning lasts from seven weeks old, when the dog's brain is fully formed, to about five months, when the dog's brain has reached a developmental threshold. Jen likens the process of young dogs learning basic cues to the relative ease with which young people learn new skills. "If you try to learn golf as an adult, as opposed to age 12, you may give up," Jen says. "It's a hard sport."

That doesn't mean older dogs can't learn, though. Outwardly, senior dogs may lack the exuberance and energy of a younger dog, but they don't lack the brainpower. Ann Allums has worked with many older dogs, some of whom had not been taught any new tricks for years. She found that the mental stimulation of a new challenge can reinvigorate an older dog. "I was teaching hand targeting to a 12-year-old dog with hip problems. Once he got the idea, he was so enthusiastic! It was like watching him get younger!" she says.

Trainer Pat Whitacre likens an older dog's learning capacity to that of learning a foreign language. A child learns a second language easily in a bilingual home, but adults can pick up a new language even if they start late. They may have an accent and not be as fluent as the child, but they'll easily learn enough to get by, he says. "It's more accurate to say that a dog has missed a *prime* window for learning," Pat says of the older dog.

Getting Started

Training starts with observation. Watch your dog carefully, even before you bring her home, to match your lessons to her needs and abilities. When does she eat, sleep, poop? What times of day is she most and least active? Is she well adjusted or exhibiting fear, anxiety, shyness, or some other negative mood that might interfere with basic training or encourage you to focus your training on overcoming her fear? Does she like food treats, or will you have to find some other way to motivate her?

Some dogs truly are blank slates, such as brand-new puppies. Others come with baggage. In Lila's case, teaching basic cues was much more difficult because she did not yet trust her trainers.

Observation led Ann to decide how to shape the initial approach to training Lila. Ann first worked on gaining Lila's trust. Then she could move on to basic manners and expanding Lila's experience of positive interactions with people.

Observing your dog to determine likes, dislikes, and behavior—in short, what makes him tick—is the first step in building a relationship. You've brought a dog home because you want a lifelong relationship with a best friend. It's important to keep that relationship in mind as you train your dog.

The Power of Positive Reinforcement

There are two basic ways to train a dog: punishing the dog for wrong behaviors, and rewarding the dog when he does right ones. Best Friends is convinced that training is most effective—and most fun—when a dog is excited about learning and when he trusts and respects the trainer. Using positive reinforcement techniques fosters this environment. Dogs, like kids, do well when they receive rewards for their achievements.

Techniques based on positive reinforcement have swept through the world of animal training since Harvard professor B. F. Skinner explained them in the mid-20th century. Skinner believed that any behavior, from a rat pressing a bar to the most creative human endeavors, is selected for by outcome and can be further reinforced through patterns of rewards. Skinner determined that complex behaviors and tasks were best learned when broken into simple steps and combined with clear cues or signals (such as a single spoken word for animals), feedback, and reinforcement with rewards immediately upon their successful demonstration. When used in a technique called "shaping," Skinner got animals to perform complex acts in return for rewards. He taught chimpanzees to spend poker chips like money to get treats, then moved on to a less complicated animal, a rat he named Pliny the Elder. Through positively reinforcing a series of simple acts, Skinner got Pliny to pull a chain to release a marble, pick up the marble, tote it across his cage, and release it into a tube.

Today, trainers using rewards in the shaping technique have taught gorillas living in zoos to docilely place their arms next to the bars of their cages to receive medical injections. They've trained law-enforcement dogs to happily seek out hidden caches of illegal drugs. Hollywood moviemakers used positive methods to get complex, desired behaviors from farm animals in the movie *Babe.*

Punishment has no place in the positive methods of shaping, capturing, or luring behavior. According to Skinner, punishment did reduce the likelihood a behavior would occur again, but it often caused even worse behaviors. He advocated avoiding punishment as a means to train animals and children.

Despite modern advances in training animals and children, old notions of "spare the rod and spoil the child" die hard. Some dog trainers jerk on collars, physically manipulate their dogs into submissive postures, and punish unwanted behavior by inflicting pain.

After a lifetime of looking for what's wrong and asking for corrections, it can be hard for an adult to even recognize good behavior, let alone reward it. Best Friends believes negative-based training is counterproductive. It erodes the relationship between human and canine. Punishment and coercion introduce fear into the learning process, and fear makes it harder for dogs to learn. Applying negative methods to mold a dog's behavior may—or may not—get you whatever you desire in the short term, but the dog will dislike training and trust you less afterward. Using negative methods may set up a further conflict over the dog's behavior later down the road, a losing situation for both involved.

"At the beginning of a new dog training class, I always tell the people, 'We're doing a positive reinforcement class,'" Jen says. "I warn them that I will start each class by asking them to name one positive thing their dog did in the previous week. And it's the hardest thing for them to do. They say what the dog did not do—that the dog didn't jump up, for example—and I say, 'Okay, you've got the right idea, but now state it positively. Turn it around, and tell us what he did do.'" She says it doesn't have to be as dramatic as the dog "learning to dial 9-1-1." It could be something as basic as keeping all four paws on the floor while he was in the kitchen, or staying quiet when a stranger came to the door. Jen recommends keeping a notebook handy (on the kitchen counter or by your bed) and writing one positive thing the dog did each day. That will help create the habit of looking for good behavior as a ticket to rewarding that behavior and making it more likely to recur.

Training by rewarding good behavior doesn't mean dogs should be allowed to do whatever they want. Dogs need a world that is predictable, with clear and consistent rules and boundaries. "It helps the dogs feel less confused and frustrated if they know the rules," Ann says. "Rules help them feel more comfortable. They want to know that there is a leader, and she's taking care of everything."

Jen adds, "If you let dogs make dog decisions, you might not like what you get." They could tear up the house, pee anywhere, dig up the yard where you don't want them to, or bark constantly. Helping them understand the rules greatly improves the human–dog relationship, which allows them to live more easily in the human world.

Rewards

Rules receive their clearest presentation when a dog learns what to do and is rewarded for it rather than avoids what not to do. For example, if you want to teach your dog to relieve herself outside, you can either teach her where to go, or teach her the dozens of places that are off-limits. Punishing the dog for urinating on the rug, the couch, the table, or the laundry doesn't provide clear instruction about where she *should* go, in the backyard or while on a walk. A dog will want to do the right thing—once you've helped her to understand what it is.

Positive training, when performed correctly, creates a strong, fun bond between dog and handler. The dog builds confidence through learning what behaviors earn the rewards from the handler. When a dog and human share good times, they form a bond that is much more solid than any forged through the human merely meeting the dog's biological needs. Such a bond doesn't emerge overnight, and that's why it's important to spend high-quality time with your dog.

To create a bond that will enrich your dog's training—as well as all other aspects of your relationship—find something you like to do together. It could be hiking, playing with a ball or flying disc, or going to training classes. If your time together is fun, the dog will want to respond to you and the training will become easier. If the training isn't fun, neither you nor the dog will want to do it, and it's likely to quickly disappear from the daily schedule.

Play, like anything else the dog enjoys, can be used as a reward in training. If your dog likes to play ball, use that to your advantage. Ask that the dog "sit," and when he does, throw the ball as a reward for successfully sitting. Through rewarding the dog by throwing the ball when he sits, he will learn to sit automatically for the ball to be thrown. Another strategy can be to work short training routines into a daily walk. For instance, you can ask your dog to sit before entering the dog park for a romp. In short, make the dog work as part of a play routine.

The dog will have to use her brain to get what she wants. She'll try to figure out how to shape human behavior—What will it take to get that bit of food?—as much as you'll think about how to shape dog behavior. The dog will enjoy the mental stimulation and problem solving in much the same way humans like to solve crossword puzzles or play word games.

The Power of Treats

Evolution has provided your dog, like all vertebrates, with hard-wiring in his upper brain stem to allow him to mate, hunt, and defend himself. Like all mammals, your dog's brain also has a limbic system to process emotion, create and store simple memories, and take part in social behaviors. But there's one crucial difference between human and dog brains. Your brain, unlike the dog's, has a large cerebral cortex to handle such higher mental functions as reason, complex language, and empathy. Nevertheless, some people attribute sophisticated thinking to a dog during training. They think the dog resists learning because she holds a grudge, or she refuses to come when called because she is stubborn. Not possible. Your dog is a pleasure–pain calculator, bent on increasing what she considers good at any given moment and minimizing what she considers bad. The dog needs to understand that obeying is better than failing to obey, and she needs a concrete reward to do that.

At Best Friends, some adopters mistakenly believe their dogs will feel thankful for being rescued and taken to their forever homes. Although the dog understands the value of a warm house and big backyard, she won't credit the adopter with the change and immediately show her gratitude by obeying every cue or signal. So, don't try to psychoanalyze your dog. If you're wondering what motivates her, look no further than such basics as eating, sleeping, and playing.

Treats can be a powerful training tool because they provide an instant reward and can be convenient to use. When a desired treat is paired over and over with a particular behavior, even the relatively simple structure of a dog's brain makes the connection. To get more treats, repeat the behavior.

Without humans to supervise them, dogs in the natural world spend most of their time trying to find enough to eat to stay alive. Dogs evolved from wolves about 15,000 years ago, thanks to a formed symbiotic relationship with humans that offered them something better than their daily grind. Getting a steadier supply of food likely helped promote that relationship.

That reward still works today. Food usually acts as a powerful motivational tool—especially if it's tasty. A bit of protein provides immediate gratification for most dogs. A treat should be soft and small, about the size of a pea, so the dog swallows it quickly and is ready for the next lesson. Soft, pasteurized cheese in an aerosol can, or what Best Friends dog trainer John Garcia calls "squeeze cheese," is a handy way to carry a lot of treats in a small package and is highly prized by many dogs in training. Other trainers find freeze-dried liver to be the champagne and caviar of dog treats.

But there's a catch. Supplementing your dog's regular daily diet with a lot of extra soft treats may provide too many calories, making your Fido a wide-o. Best Friends trainers recommend considering how to creatively turn a dog's dinner into a daylong training tool rather than increase his caloric intake with additional treats. Instead of feeding your dog all at once, you could start the day by measuring your dog's daily ration, including any special treats, into a container. Give the dog some of the contents as you train him. As long as food is available, you can choose to use it as a training reward, a snack, or a separate meal. Just be sure the container is empty at the end of the day. An added bonus is that hand-feeding your dog in response to good behavior strengthens your relationship.

Finding Your Dog's Reward

Some trainers at Best Friends joke that all you need to train a dog are patience and a pocketful of chicken. That's not always true though. Some dogs don't respond to food. For them, a reward might be a toy, a scratch, or verbal praise. Only the dog gets to decide what constitutes a reward. That's why training has to begin with careful observation.

"When I worked at the shelter [in Minnesota], we had dogs that came in who were too nervous to eat," Jen says. "Their stomachs were in knots. So we'd have to find a toy or something else to treat them. Just like people, all dogs are different, and different things motivate different dogs. That's what's cool about Best Friends. We treat the dogs as individuals. We don't say, 'Oh, you're a herding dog, so you must love to herd sheep.' No, we get to know the dog first."

Whatever the dog's reward turns out to be, it must be given immediately upon successful completion of a desired behavior for the dog to make the correct causal connection. Jen recalls a frustrated call from a dog adopter who had too big of a gap between action and reward. The owner was trying to housetrain the dog, but things weren't going right. "I said, tell me what you do," Jen recalls. The owner said, "Well, we go outside, he potties, we come inside, and he sits next to the treat drawer." Jen realized the dog was being rewarded not for relieving himself in the yard, but for going inside and sitting afterward. "You probably have a dog who wants to go out all the time, because he gets treats when he comes back in," she told him.

A more effective use of food as a reward in housetraining would be to go outside with the dog and reward him with a treat right after (within 1–3 seconds) he potties. Whatever the dog does right before the treat is given is what the dog will associate with the treat!

A Good Routine

Ever see a dog begin to pace and paw as suppertime rolls around? Most dogs like to live by a routine. Regular times for walks, meals, play, and sleep seem to reassure them and keep them calm. Nervous dogs in particular, including many adopted from Best Friends, are

Clicker Training
Dime-store clicking toys, also called "clickers" or "crickets," have been shown to accelerate learning in dogs. Renowned animal trainer Karen Pryor pinpoints their introduction to a 1992 seminar in San Francisco that brought together animal trainers and behavioral scientists. One presenter, dog trainer Gary Wilkes, had bought some plastic crickets at a novelty shop, picking up on a 1960 idea of B. F. Skinner's that they thought could be used effectively with dogs. The sharp *pop-pop* or *click-click* the toys make when squeezed acts like a behavioral snapshot, freezing in the dog's mind exactly what she was doing when the click occurred. Trainers click at the moment the dog exhibits the desired behavior and then give a treat, creating by association what behaviorists call a "conditioned reinforcer."

The click acts as a "bridging stimulus," tying together the two acts of the dog winning the treat and the dog receiving the treat. Once the dog understands what made the owner pop the clicker, she seeks to make it happen again.

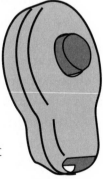

Ask the dog to do something. Click once, in the instant the dog's body is exactly where it should be. Then give one treat. Don't overclick. It's a tool best used with discrimination.

grounded in knowing what to expect every day. If training sessions truly are fun for dog and owner, the dog will look forward to them.

If possible, it's easier on both partners in the training relationship to have short sessions throughout the day, rather than one long session in the evening. Dogs have short attention spans, with puppies unable to concentrate for more than a few seconds. So, ten one-minute sessions probably are better than one ten-minute session. Puppies should not be asked to repeat a cued behavior more than two or three times; that's all they can handle at one sitting. In addition, training that falls in one large block can become a burden. The owner may skip a night and pledge to do a session twice as long the next day, but that rarely happens. Training times that are short, fun, and easy to fit into a schedule are more likely than marathon sessions to be repeated—and repetition equals results. In addition to a specific routine for training, with scheduled times, remember your dog is learning how to act every moment of the day. Regardless of what the clock says, be ready to make any moment an opportunity for behavior modification.

Professional Help

You love your dog and want to do what's best for him. Trouble is, you may not know how to get the best behavior out of your dog while maintaining your loving, positive relationship. That's where a trainer comes in. Best Friends recommends finding a good trainer to help you, especially if the dog has particular issues that you're struggling to rectify. In the end, though, the decision on how to train rests on the individual dogs and owners. Some people have an affinity for working with dogs and may enjoy figuring things out for themselves, especially if their dogs are well-adjusted and don't have socialization problems. Others need a little help. Jen likens the situation to the way people act when they bring home a new piece of electronic equipment. Some read the instruction manual line by line. Some prefer to try to get the equipment working on their own, exploring each button and circuit by trial and error. And some, no matter how much they try to figure things out, need to call the manufacturer's hotline. Nearly anyone can teach a simple "Sit." For training dogs to perform more complicated behaviors (and for knowing what steps to take if your dog develops serious behavior issues, see Chapter 8), an in-home or group demonstration might be necessary.

In addition to expert advice on training, group training classes allow dogs to socialize, as well as to learn how to work around distractions. When dogs meet other dogs and people, they begin to lose their fear of new encounters.

You have a lot of options to find a trainer who's right for you and your dog. You can go online and search for expert dog trainers. If you go this route, Best Friends recommends websites including the Association of Pet Dog Trainers (www.apdt.com) and Karen Pryor's Clicker Training (www.clickertraining.com). Websites that rate training services, with feedback posted by customers, can be useful, as can advertisements in phone books. Many fine trainers belong to groups you can find in published and online guides, but you should always use these resources as a starting point for personal inquiries, much the same way employers read stacks of job applications but interview the top candidates. Word-of-mouth endorsements from friends who have well-behaved dogs can be particularly effective. When you've got a prospective trainer in mind, ask about training methods and whether the trainer uses positive training methods. Better yet, ask if you can observe a training session. If you find the trainer using force or you otherwise feel uncomfortable, then it's not the right fit for you and your dog.

A Common Language: Cues and Signals

Understand the benefits of training from the day you bring your dog home. Some owners don't begin to work with their dogs until behaviors get out of hand and need correcting. Better to avoid problems by training in the first place.

Start your training by talking with everyone in your home and agreeing on a list of cue words ("cue" is the term Best Friends prefers to the notion of giving a dog a "command"). One person should begin the training, but all eventually should take turns to get the dog to generalize the cues and get used to taking cues from different people. To add variety to the dog's training schedule, try having one person lead the sessions in the morning and another in the afternoon or evening. Or have one person work with the dog until she masters a behavior, and then have a second person work on the same one.

Common short cues for behavior appear below, but you don't have to follow these terms rigidly. After all, an English bulldog doesn't speak English any more than a French poodle speaks French. Cues and signals have no meaning to a dog until paired with specific behaviors and reinforced with rewards. If your dog won't sit when told to do so, it's because you haven't made the sound "Sit" have any meaning. Calmly work through your routines again instead of acting like the stereotypical tourist in a foreign country, raising your voice and speaking slowly in hopes of being better understood.

You may find that adopted dogs have negative associations with certain words. Jen recalls working with a rescue dog who cringed whenever he heard the word *come*. You can use any cue word or phrase you want—she said you could even use "Peanut butter and jelly," but she settled on "Here" with the anxious dog—as long as you pair the term with the behavior you have positively reinforced.

Setting Up Your Sessions

Expert animal trainer Karen Pryor, author of *Don't Shoot the Dog!*, finds that an animal will respond to as many as 80 reinforcements in one day. Be prepared before your training session begins. Cut up a hot dog into bites the size of a pea, or tear up commercially prepared doggie treats into enough tiny bits to fill a plastic sandwich bag or a jar in a handy place. Reward your dog the instant she follows your instructions, not five or ten seconds later. Remember, she will associate the reward with whatever she was doing just prior to receiving it.

As your dog progresses through more challenging tasks, you may need to rely on your higher-quality treats, such as freeze-dried liver, to teach her new behaviors and reward her strongest performances.

 **Easy Training Times** You don't have to set aside a half hour each night just for dog training. Best Friends recommends slipping in a few training exercises when you've got a moment of free time. Try these:

• during commercials on television. Mute the sound and work on getting your dog to come or do "doggie push-ups" (see page 138).

• while waiting for water to boil on the stovetop or in the microwave.

• while waiting for the computer to print a long document.

• while your morning toast is browning.

• as part of a walk or trip to the dog park.

• while you're giving the clothes an extra few minutes in the dryer.

Lower-value treats can be used to maintain the skills your dog is already fluent in.

The duration and frequency of training sessions will depend on your dog and your schedule. Some dogs get bored quickly; some want to continue lessons all day. Others may get more out of a series of short bursts scattered throughout the day. As a rule, puppies have shorter attention spans than adult dogs. Adolescent dogs of, say, six months to a year, like teenagers, are developing so fast that they may need remedial lessons. Contrary to the adage about old dogs balking at new tricks, dog brains have as much plasticity as those of their human partners and are quite capable of mastering new lessons.

Luring Versus Capturing

You'll want to decide whether to lure the dog into the behavior you want, to "capture" it as it occurs naturally, or to do both. Another method of behavior modification, physical prompting, has a long history but isn't always positive or pleasant. It involves pushing and pulling your dog into desired positions, such as a sit. Such prompting or modeling has two main drawbacks. First, it often is dangerous or abusive with dogs who have socialization issues; they may respond with fight or flight. Second, physical prompting is impossible when the dog is off leash. Just try forcing your dog to come to you—good luck!—when she's a hundred yards away and chasing a squirrel.

Luring involves using a treat to get a dog to move her body into a position for her reward. Capturing requires you to wait for the dog to perform some desired behavior on her own and then reward it. If you watch your dog out of the corner of your eye, you will notice when she starts to sit. Reward as her rump hits the floor.

Some behavior is hard to lure but easy to capture. For example, one Best Friends trainer gave rewards for sneezing; the dog soon learned the connection.

Luring and capturing require patience. Don't attempt to train the dog when you're tired or grumpy because you will not be at your best and the session will become compromised. Likewise, don't try to force the dog into training when her heart's not in it. Plan to end the lesson before it becomes drudgery for you or the dog; finish with your dog still wanting more.

Places and Spaces

Begin your training in a part of your home that is quiet and relatively free of distractions. Competing sounds, actions, and animals will interfere with your dog's ability to concentrate. A quiet living room or kitchen should work fine. Note that a second dog almost always presents a distraction; if you have two new dogs, you'll likely have to train them one at a time.

Many dogs have trouble generalizing. They may learn to sit in the kitchen but are slow to transfer the behavior anywhere else. They also must learn to generalize to the difference in humans as well as their environment. To start promoting generalization of behavior, shift the training around the inside of the house, and move to the patio and driveway.

Vary the time and duration of the training too. After your dog masters an action at close range, vary the duration, distance, and distractions during your session. For instance, to vary the duration for the behaviors of "Sit" and "Down," slowly increase elapsed time before giving the reward. To add distance, try moving a step away from the dog and giving the cue. To add distractions during training, try making noises or dropping objects. Ask a friend or family member to walk by when your dog is in a sit, and reward the dog if he is able to resist the distraction.

When the dog has mastered your cues, you'll slowly want to alter the reward system of one treat per act. You can't very well tote a bag of treats with you every moment of every day. Shift from one act, one reward, to a system where the dog gets rewards at random times. Keep praising the dog for each behavior performed on cue.

Once in a while in return for a particularly good response from the dog—such as coming very quickly when called—give the dog a "jackpot" reward that is bigger and better than anything she has received before. You'll quickly turn your dog into the equivalent of a gambler at a Las Vegas slot machine: The dog is addicted to performing the same actions over and over in hopes of payouts that range from small to large.

Start a particular lesson by getting your dog's attention. Any sound or motion that prompts a response will do, but Best Friends trainers prefer using the dog's name. So for practical reasons, your first lesson may be to get your dog to recognize her name.

Name Recognition

A dog's recognition of her own name is an important part of a successful training routine. Saying her name breaks the dog away from what she is doing to refocus her attention on you. For example, saying "Mindy!" sets up the dog to focus on "Sit," or whatever cue follows next.

It's easy to get a brand-new puppy to learn her name. Just say the name and immediately deliver the treat without regard for any response to the sound. Repeat that action many times over the course of several days. That will get the dog to associate the sound of her name with good things, priming her to want to respond when she hears her name aloud. Ideally, you'll be able to stop whatever the dog is doing, even running away from you, just by saying her name aloud. If you've adopted a new dog and want to change her name, the process is the same: Say the name. Give a treat. Repeat.

Don't show the treat first. Use the treat as a reward. Ann Allums uses the analogy of your salary as motivation for a week's work. You get paid after you're done, not before, so why shouldn't your dog be the same way? Your dog can learn the same. She associates the treat with successfully completing the requested action.

Once the dog recognizes her name, Jen Severud cautions against its overuse. Pair the name with clear instructions, and avoid speaking the name just to say it. If you say the dog's name over and over again, you run the risk of the dog learning to ignore the sound of her name.

Name Recognition

GOAL: Five to ten times per session

1 Have a treat ready.

2 Say the dog's name, and reward with a treat.

Sit

"Sit" is an easy behavior for dogs to learn, and one of the first a dog should master. A dog naturally sits from time to time, and you can capture the behavior by offering a reward when his rear end touches the floor.

Another tactic is to lure the dog into the proper position with a treat. Think of the lure as a magnet and your dog as a compass needle. Hold the treat in front of the dog's nose, just beyond his reach. Slowly move the treat over the top of the dog's head toward his tail. His head will swing up to follow the path of the treat, and his rear end will go down. When the dog's rear end rests flat on the floor, give the treat. Wait until the dog reliably offers the behavior before introducing the verbal cue "Sit."

If the dog jumps up for the treat, you're holding it too high. If the dog backs away from you instead of sitting, try again after positioning the dog so he's right in front of a wall or corner and cannot retreat.

As you practice, have the dog maintain the sit for only a second or two. It's helpful to stand right in front of the dog. Give the dog the treat, and then release him with a simple verbal cue, such as "OK." The release cue tells the dog when he can stop doing the behavior.

Once the dog has learned to reliably maintain a sit, try the cue in many different places, both inside and out, and gradually add distractions. Try gradually teaching your dog to hold the sit for longer and longer periods of time. To increase the duration of the sit, wait a second or two longer before giving the reward. Watch your dog's reactions and see if you can slowly extend how long he sits before being rewarded; slow down if the dog gets frustrated or it appears as if you're asking for more behavior than he feels the treat is worth.

Sit **GOAL:** Three "Sits" per session

1 Without speaking, hold the leash in one hand and a treat in the other.

2 Keeping the treat within inches of the dog's nose, lure the dog into a sitting position by moving the treat backward over the dog's head (toward his tail).

3 Continue moving the treat toward the dog's tail. When the dog rocks back into a sit, reward with treat and praise.

Down

"Down" is an excellent cue to get an excited dog to settle. Start with the dog in the sitting position in front of you. Hold the treat in front of his nose and slowly lower it to the floor. The dog may take a while to lie on the floor, so be patient and keep trying. As the dog puts belly and chest to the floor while keeping his rear end down flat on the floor, give the treat with praise. Don't pull down on the dog's collar, as this will likely cause the dog to resist. Pushing or pulling constitutes physical modeling and could produce the problems already identified with this technique.

You might consider capturing a "Down" instead of luring into it. Getting down on the belly from a sit may be easier if you bring the dog's bed into the training area. She may naturally move into a down position.

Jen demonstrates how luring can be taught to a young adult, mixed-breed dog named Shirley, who's fairly new to Best Friends. Shirley, black with white socks, offered a sit when Jen stood nearby. That earned a "click" and a tasty treat (see "Clicker Training," page 125). Jen then tried to lure Shirley to the floor. She hesitated for several moments and then slid her belly to the floor. Jen responded with three treats, a bounty intended to demonstrate just how good it is for Shirley to stay down. "She doesn't want to get up," Jen says. "She's got a good thing here."

Stand

Once you have the dog sitting or lying down, place a treat in front of the dog's snout and slowly move it straight out and away from her nose. The treat acts like a magnet, drawing the dog toward the treat and requiring her to stand as she follows it.

Down GOAL: Three "Downs" per session

1 Begin with the dog in the "Sit" position. Without speaking, hold the leash in one hand and a treat in the other.

2 Lure the dog into a "Down" position by slowly moving the treat toward the ground, keeping the treat within inches of the dog's nose.

3 When the dog follows the lure into a "Down" position, reward with a treat and praise.

Sit From Down

Start with the dog in the down position. Hold a treat in front of and just above her nose. Raise the treat slowly over the dog's head. This will attract the dog toward a sit. Follow up with the treat when she reaches the sitting position.

You may want to put your dog through "doggie push-ups" to get her comfortable with recognizing the variety of cues and moving her from one position to another. "Doggie push-ups" are simply a matter of having your dog go from a sit to a down and then back to a sit. You should vary when you give a treat, so the dog doesn't learn to predict that he only gets a treat after sit or only after down during doggie push-ups. Try to get your dog to do a sit-down-sit with one reward at the end.

Come

Being able to reliably call your dog to your side is probably the most important cue. It's the key to having a successful relationship with your dog when he is off leash. When your dog learns that good things happen when he returns upon hearing the "Come" cue, you will be able to remove him from potentially bad situations. You could even save his life.

Getting a dog to reliably return to you depends on three key factors:

1 You must make coming to you as much fun as possible. You may find you have to raise the quality of treats you give as rewards. Realistically, your rewards may not always be more powerful than every distraction your dog may encounter.

2 You must avoid pairing "Come" with something the dog perceives as bad. If you only use "Come" at the dog park when you are ready to leave, the dog quickly will learn that coming back to you produces an unpleasant outcome: no more fun! The dog is, in fact, penalized for coming to you, and less likely to return in the future. To avoid this problem, call the dog with the "Come" cue several times during fun times together, rewarding each time, and then send him out to play some more. At home, don't use "Come" when you need to do something the dog won't like, such as clipping toenails or giving a bath. In those cases, simply find your dog and gently lead him where you want him to go. Don't forget to use positive rewards to put some fun into the unpleasant task.

❸ You must not overuse the word *come,* particularly if you cannot enforce the dog's return to you. If you say "Come, come, come," and the dog refuses to respond, the word begins to lose its meaning. Best Friends has found that some dogs have ignored the word for so long that trainers have to come up with a new word to use for the desired behavior, such as "Here."

To lay a good foundation for this behavior, begin teaching this cue in a relatively distraction-free environment, such as inside your home. You can wait until the dog comes to you on his own and capture the behavior, or you can prompt your dog to approach.

Start by having the dog on a standard leash and his favorite treats or toys in your hands. Get the dog excited about what you're holding, and then step backward and say, "Come." The dog likely will follow you to receive the reward.

Another way to get your dog to come to you is to behave in ways that arouse his curiosity. Try squatting without bending at the waist. Your dog will likely want to check out why you're on his level. Another option is to run away from your dog. His instinct to chase probably will make him follow you. Once the dog gets close, stop, turn, and squat to receive the dog. As the dog nears you, say "Come" and give the treat when he reaches your body. You should fill your voice with enthusiasm and smile to indicate your pleasure. As you practice the cue, try it from a variety of rooms at random times throughout the day.

In the early stages of teaching, Best Friends trainers recommend that your dog always be on a leash and never allowed to fail. She should be rewarded when she comes to the spot where you gave the cue, whether she walks there on her own or you have to walk to her and "jolly" her back with you. "Come" should always result in good times with no opportunity for the dog to begin making wrong decisions.

After you've practiced the cue indoors, go outside to your yard or to a park. You'll want to make sure your dog cannot ignore the cue, so keep her on a 20- to 30-foot leash. Let the dog wander, sniffing and exploring the ground around you, until her attention is focused on something. Then get her attention by making a novel sound, such as clapping, stomping, or squeaking a toy. You can use her name, but only say it once or else she may begin to ignore it. When she looks at you, squat or run away to prompt the behavior she has practiced indoors. As she nears you and appears to be about to reach you, give the "come" cue, followed by a treat. Keep repeating, with treats each time she follows through.

If your dog ignores you, don't reel him in like a fish. That activates the dog's reflex to pull back. Instead, go to the dog and, in an excited manner, lead him back to where you called. Sometimes as you move closer to the dog, he decides to move toward you. Act cheerful—you're not punishing him—and finish with the verbal cue and reward. After you've worked on the long leash and your dog has a consistent recall, you can move to a shorter leash. Let

Come GOAL: Three "Comes" per session

1 Start with the dog on a leash in one hand and her favorite reward in the other. Call the dog's name, and then show the reward you are holding.

2 When your dog is interested in the object, take a step backward and give the cue, "Come."

3 When the dog moves toward you, reward with treats and praise. If your dog does not move forward, do not repeat the cue. Lure her to you with the reward.

Gradually increase the distance for the "Come" until you are using a 20-foot line and getting consistent returns.

your dog drag a six-foot leash around the yard while you practice getting his attention and calling him to you. When he understands that "Come" means treats and positive attention, he will be more reliable about returning to you when prompted.

Once the dog comes reliably on leash, set him free in a fenced area and try again without the physical restraint. If he refuses to come when called, stop issuing the cue. If you repeat the cue without eliciting the desired behavior, your dog will quickly learn that he only has to obey when he feels like it. Or, like a child repeatedly called home by parents at dinner time, the dog will figure out that the cue can be safely ignored the first few times it's given. If the dog isn't ready to come to you while off leash, take a step back in your training and practice with the dog on the leash again.

Although not technically part of the "Come" training, you will want to encourage your dog to keep track of you even when she wanders off leash. One way to build this owner-tracking behavior is to play hide and seek. When your dog is distracted inside a fenced area, hide. Make a noise to attract her attention, or just wait until she realizes you are gone and tries to find you. When she does find you, praise and reward her. Practicing this little game teaches the dog that good things happen when she keeps track of you. If you do this often enough, your dog may never let you out of sight.

Going on a Walk

Unless you plan to compete in the Iditarod or need help getting up a steep driveway, you'll prefer a dog who doesn't pull. Tugging can be annoying, and in the case of large and powerful dogs, downright dangerous. The right equipment can encourage the dog not to pull and reduce the strength needed to work with the dog. These include front-clip and other no-pull harnesses and head halters, as described in Chapter 4 (see page 106). Best Friends has many volunteers walking dogs and uses specially designed harnesses to discourage pulling. They're not solutions in themselves, but rather tools to use while teaching your dog not to pull. Whether they work or not is up to the dog—all dogs are individuals—and what one animal gently accepts may cause another to buck and fight.

Regardless of whether you need special harnesses or halters, your goal is "loose leash" walking. To anyone who has said the magic word *Walk!* and watched a dog dance in delight, it's no secret that going for a walk is a reward in itself. If the dog pulls on the leash while walking, he will view the reward of the walk as proper compensation for the pulling. Your pulling back likely will only make the dog pull harder and ignore you. To get the dog to walk with a slack leash, make him understand that walks only occur when he's not pulling.

It's so easy, it literally is child's play. Just imagine you're playing red light, green light. When the leash is loose, keep walking and praising your dog. As soon as the dog tugs, stop and be silent. The dog will want to know why you've stopped and will return to you, putting slack back in the leash. Resume the walk and give plenty of praise until the leash goes tight again. Repeat with halting silence. Soon enough, you will be able to take more than one step at a time before having to stop again as the dog puts two and two together and maintains a loose leash for longer periods. Plan your walks for time, not distance. In the beginning, you may move only 30 feet in a 20-minute walk because of your constant stopping. Later, you may cover a mile.

You'll have to be consistent with this training tip. Don't let the dog pull once in a while, because she'll figure that if it works sometimes, it's worth trying all the time. Also, don't expect the dog to continue walking nonstop. Sniffing provides mental stimulation. A dog reading the trails of other animals is like humans analyzing stories in a newspaper or magazine.

Wait

Use this cue to get your dog to pause before moving forward. Start with a closed doorway to block your dog's movement. Then progress to a partially open door, and then a fully opened door, as the dog's skill improves. This makes it possible for nearly any person to block any dog. As you cross the threshold, tell your dog, "Wait" and hold your open hand in front of his face as a visual cue, or physically block the dog with your body in the doorway. The dog should wait on the other side of the door and not try to move through the doorway until you release him from the wait. Step through the door and pause. Then use your release word, like "OK," and allow the dog to cross the threshold. You may reward the dog for waiting patiently, although some Best Friends trainers consider going through the doorway its own reward and prefer not to use treats.

"Wait" is a fairly easy cue to teach if you body-block the dog because dogs use that behavior on one another, physically preventing one another from moving to a specific place. This is a great cue to use when you want the dog to wait at any open door. For example, the dog needs to learn to wait inside the car after you open the door to snap on her leash.

Leave It

Imagine: You're taking your dog for a walk on a bright fall afternoon. You see a gray mass on the sidewalk, and as you approach,

144

Wait GOAL: Three "Waits" per session

1 Approach a door with your dog on leash. Cue your dog to sit.

2 Slowly open the door. If your dog starts to get up out of the sit and/or move forward, calmly close the door or step in front of him to block the way through the door. Start again at the beginning with the sit, until your dog does not move forward to the door when you open it.

3 After the dog holds his sit, give a release word ("OK," "Free," "Release"), at which time your dog can proceed through the doorway. The dog should not move toward the door until you give the release cue.

you realize it's a dead squirrel. To you, it's probably pretty disgusting. To your dog, the dead animal's scent is a source of infinite fascination. How to get her to ignore the sight and smell she finds so alluring?

Best Friends trainers will tell you, it's hard. The dog wants to check out what she sees and smells, and if you use the tools of positive reinforcement, you have to have a reward for the dog that trumps what's on the ground before her. Ann recommends a little stage managing. Start by placing a dry dog biscuit on the ground as bait. As your dog discovers the biscuit, say "Leave it." Because your dog will naturally want to investigate the item on the floor, when first teaching the behavior, you must be prepared to stand between the dog and the biscuit, or cover the biscuit with a foot. As soon as she takes her attention off the biscuit, produce a juicy piece of hot dog, or some other higher-quality treat. Reward the dog and praise in a happy voice. The idea is not to punish the dog for going toward a temptation, but rather to have her realize that the words "Leave it" mean that something much better awaits from you.

Only practice this lesson when you can manage the environment and ensure that the dog cannot get to the "Leave it" object. A higher-value reward for ignoring the temptation, combined with no success in getting it, create the best conditions for a strong "Leave it" habit. Try to make "Leave it" an anticipatory cue; use it before she gets diverted by distractions.

Housetraining

With vigilance, your dog should never have an accident in the house. It's an old joke among dog trainers: If your dog does make a mess, (1) get a newspaper and roll it up, and (2) hit yourself over the head and say, "Bad owner! Bad! What kind of silly owner would let that happen?" If your dog does have an accident in the house, the blame rests squarely on your shoulders.

Luckily, successful housetraining has just three steps. First, make sure the dog is never in a position to do the wrong thing. Second, make sure the dog is where she needs to be when she does have to go. Third, praise and reward your dog for getting it right.

Housetraining starts with keeping the dog under constant supervision. This may mean closing off part of the house so the dog can't wander away, confining the dog to a crate, or keeping the dog on a leash attached to you while you are inside.

Try to anticipate when your dog will need to relieve herself. For puppies, elimination happens often. Very young puppies need to be taken to their toilet at least once an hour. The rule of thumb is that puppies can hold their bladders for the number of hours that equals their age in months, plus one. For instance, a four-month-old puppy has to pee after five hours. Puppies tend to urinate within 30 seconds of waking up, and defecate a minute or two after that.

With older dogs, they may demonstrate several behaviors when they're ready to go. By closely observing your dog, you eventually will read her signs for imminent elimination. They might include sniffing, circling, pacing, squatting, or some other idiosyncrasy of your particular dog. As the dog begins to recognize that you register her signs, she may try to get your attention. At that point, say something to get her revved up, such as "Want to go outside?" At that point, lead her to the yard.

Don't be tense when you're waiting for your dog to go potty, as the dog may sense your nervousness and may not be able to relax enough to relieve herself. If the dog doesn't go right away, take her back indoors. Put her in a crate or on leash, or take whatever other measures you normally do to eliminate all opportunities to pee indoors. After five or ten minutes, take her out again. Repeat until she relieves herself outdoors. Doing so will encourage the dog that being outside is the time and place to go potty.

Once the dog has learned to go to the toilet outdoors, you can let her out into the yard to do her business or let her take bathroom breaks on a walk. Some people speed the process by training the dog to relieve herself as soon as she goes outside, and then save the walk as a reward. That system may eliminate the need to take plastic bags on the walk and carry the dog's fecal matter home for disposal.

If your dog begins to relieve herself in the house while you are watching, interrupt her with a startling noise, such as a clap of the hands or the sound "Eh-eh." The point is not to traumatize the dog, but merely to stop the behavior. Then immediately take her outside on her leash and wait for what comes naturally. If the dog is having problems with inappropriate elimination, you may want to check to see if the dog has any medical issues interfering with her training. (That's good advice for any problem you have difficulty correcting; see Chapter 7 for troubleshooting on unwanted behaviors.)

Keeping It Fun

All of the lessons in this chapter help you and your dog learn fundamental manners and help the two of you bond in the process of learning together. You'll see what motivates your dog, what kinds of training sessions work best for him, and what kinds of things you can do together to have more fun. Your dog's brain will be challenged and engaged by training, resulting in a happier, more well-adjusted dog.

Top Tips

•Only your dog gets to decide what constitutes a reward for him. See what rings your dog's bell and use that as the treat.

•When food is used as a reward, be calorie-conscious. Too many food treats in addition to a dog's regular meals can pack on the pounds.

•Determine what your list of training cues will be before you begin teaching. All people in the house involved in training the dog should know and use these terms.

•Have regular sessions that fit your schedule every day. Tailor the length and intensity to your dog's level of interest and attention span.

•Have fun. Teaching sessions should be an enjoyable experience for both of you. If you're not having fun, you're not doing it right!

Fur flying, Sylvie and her doggy friends enjoy a brisk walk with trainer Ann Allums. Exercise is a great way to bond and to keep your dog happy and fit.

Exercise
and Enrichment

It's not enough to teach your dog proper behavior. Your dog is itching to learn so much more, and recreation can help scratch that itch. Like humans, dogs get enormous benefits from mental and physical enrichment throughout their lives. Challenging their brains and bodies improves their quality of life and cements the bond between dogs and humans.

On the flip side, a dog who's not enjoying an enriched life can become bored, depressed, and physically ill. An unhappy dog may find creative and destructive ways to bring sunshine into his darkened life. He may bark constantly, destroy household objects, chew on himself, and not be responsive to people. Like humans, dogs can shut down.

It's also not enough to merely walk your dog and give him toys. Although dogs appreciate routines—who hasn't seen a dog remind her human companion when it's dinnertime?—they also thrive on new experiences. The same walk and play, day after day, provides a foundation of physical and mental stimulation. Enriching activities, however, keep a dog sharp and more richly connected to her environment and her family. Enrichment encourages dogs to be all they can be.

The key time to begin enrichment activities is during a puppy's prime socialization period, from 7 to about 14 weeks of age. Dogs are more open to accepting new situations during this window of opportunity as their brains forge billions of neural connections. That doesn't mean you can't begin enrichment activities later in a dog's life. It may only mean that first you must work with your older dog to overcome fear of new things. Dogs approach enrichment activities from their own comfort levels, making enrichment mean different things to different dogs. For a shy, undersocialized dog, an introduction to enrichment might be as simple as walking different paths from day to day, or entering one of the octagonal housing units at Dogtown for the first time. For an outgoing, confident dog, enrichment could include complicated behaviors such as the sports of doggie freestyle or agility.

"Dogs need variety," says Best Friends dog trainer Jen Severud. "We get in a rut sometimes too. We go for a walk, and at the end of the driveway, the dog automatically turns to go one way. Well, what happens if you pick another route? It might challenge his brain if you do something different." Such mental stimulation is just as important as physical exercise.

Karina, who came to Best Friends as a stray, lives for novelty. "She is one of the type who doesn't do well here because she is so stinking smart," Jen says.

Karina initially wasn't happy with her life behind a fence. For a long time, she ran a set course through her run at Dogtown, wearing a track into the dirt. That's a routine that didn't benefit her. She wasn't being mentally challenged by her environment; she was merely burning nervous energy. Jen decided to change that. She blocked the dog's usual track with a bit of fencing, and then watched Karina make her rounds. The dog had become so accustomed to her daily routines that she smacked into the fence as if it weren't there. Only then did she realize something new occupied her pen and she would have to adapt. Jen tries to vary the location of the fencing from time to time, to keep a dog who's too bright to enjoy a dull routine, guessing and learning. Best Friends trainer Ann Allums has also taught Karina some impressive tricks such as how to push a videotape into a VCR with her nose and turn on light switches with her paw. Keeping Karina's mind, as well as her body, engaged has led to a more contented dog.

Finding good forms of enrichment requires you to understand your dog's likes and dislikes. Some dogs want to run, pull, herd, or play. Some require a lot of physical stimulation, whereas others don't need as much. All need to be mentally challenged.

Jen, who has a Siberian husky, knows the breed typically gets satisfaction from running several miles a day, but that's not something she is prepared to do. "I have bad knees," she says. "I don't run unless I'm being chased or I'm late. So, I have to do things to keep her busy, or else she gets bored and may get into mischief." So each day Jen brings her husky to the office, where her dog can interact with other people and dogs rather than sleep all day long at home.

An active dog like Jen's also benefits from a large, fenced-in yard and the opportunity to pull things, which is part of a Siberian's natural inclination. When Jen put a sled dog harness on her dog, her dog reacted as if she had been born to pull a sled. Such a dog might enjoy pulling a human on roller blades or on a bicycle, if she's safely connected to the bike. Jen recommends getting your dog used to pulling on a sled dog harness while you are on foot before proceeding to having your dog pull you on a bike or rollerblades. Make sure you obtain the proper pulling equipment to keep both you and your dog safe.

Indoor Fun

It's good to have a repertoire of indoor enrichment activities. Not only do they help settle an excitable dog, but they also may be just what you need when a dog can't go outside. As a Minnesotan, Jen has firsthand knowledge of the benefits of indoor games.

"I had to be creative with my clients in Minnesota, because if we had a week of below-zero temperatures, it could be dangerous to walk outside," she says. "My dogs were inside and going bonkers. They needed something to do. So we came up with things they could do in the house, like scent work or the find-it game. That's where you put the dog out of the room, hide kibble or small treats, and systematically lead the dog around to find them." Jen notes there's a bit of mental challenge for human game players as well—they have to remember where they hid everything. Twenty minutes of such activities indoors can be just as tiring for a dog as a brisk walk, she says.

The find-it game blends the dog's natural desire to locate food with her desire to track down the source of smells. Try dropping a piece or two of your dog's food into each container of a muffin tin. This will force the dog to go from cup to cup and make it impossible to gulp her food. Or take a handful of kibble and scatter it on the floor. Your dog will enjoy tracking down each piece, and the activity will keep her occupied for a while. Don't try this if you have other dogs who are food aggressive. Also, try hiding kibble in a cardboard box or inside two paper bags. Let the dog tear through the bag or box to get to the food inside.

Ann takes dogs to indoor venues other than her home in winter. Pet stores that allow dogs inside offer plenty of interesting smells. Dogs enjoy exploring the aisles, sniffing the food and treats, and seeing other dogs. They get the added bonus of becoming more confident and comfortable around other dogs.

"I have noticed that with my dogs, the more places I take them, the more at ease they are everywhere, so I can take them more places," Ann says.

Don't forget that spending time with your dog, indoors or out, will be rewarding to the dog no matter what you do. Ann says some volunteers at Best Friends read to the dogs at the sanctuary. They may enjoy hearing a human voice and receiving attention, even though they don't understand the words being spoken.

Toys: Many dogs find playing with toys a great way to pass the time. Hard but chewable Kong toys have an odd shape that makes them bounce in unpredictable ways. They force dogs to pay close attention to catch them.

Stuffing these toys with food makes them doubly attractive to dogs. If you mix peanut butter, dry dog food, and a little broth, you can spoon the mixture into the Kong's hollow center, and freeze it. Your dog will enjoy gnawing it as it thaws, eagerly trying to get at the food inside. If you've got an overweight dog, substitute low-fat cream cheese for the peanut butter or water for the broth. (For more on puzzle toys and food toys, see "Food Toys" in Chapter 4, page 104.)

Chewing on a frozen Kong promotes self-discipline. "When a puppy is chewing on a Kong, she is lying down and learning how to settle, be calm, and think," Ann says. "She's directing that energy, staying focused."

Other good chew toys to keep a dog's attention include raw beef bones, bully sticks, and animal antlers. Raw bones are best for a dog's teeth and digestion, and they won't splinter as easily as cooked bones.

Games for Dogs and People: A dog finds some enrichment simply by being with other dogs. Many dogs create their own games: They chase each other, tease each other, wrestle, and play tug.

Shaggy, an appropriately named rescue dog who looks like a Muppet, likes to play three-way tug-of-war with other dogs at Best Friends. Often, when dogs play together in a pen at Best Friends, Jen will give them a rope so they can play tug with each other. It's good exercise not only when they pull, but also when one dog gets the rope all to himself. That often sets off a chase as other dogs try to take it away.

Tug-of-war also is a good indoor game for a human and a dog. First, teach your dog a cue like "Drop it," rather than prying an object out of your dog's mouth. Teach "Drop it" by putting a treat in front of the dog's nose and giving him the treat when he releases the object. For tug-of-war, use a sturdy rope or tug toy.

A good game of tug has rules that must be followed. Make sure to teach the dog that the game ends if he puts his teeth on your flesh or mouths your hands, and that he must release the rope upon receiving the cue. Stop playing tug while the dog still is interested, so you build the dog's enthusiasm for the next time you choose to play.

You also can get a dog to chase you, indoors or out. In fact, one of the best ways to teach a dog to come to you is to run away from him. The dog's instinct is to chase something moving away, so he is likely to follow where you go. If you hide, your dog probably will try to seek you out. Jen says she once let a dog off a leash and discovered to her chagrin that he did not want to come back. So she hid behind a bush, and he came to her.

A Game of Tug

Tug should be a safe outlet for your dog's natural energy. If at any time during the game your dog's teeth touch your skin or clothing, immediately make a startling noise ("Ouch!") and end the game. Even if the dog did not mean to touch your skin, ending the game will help teach the dog to be careful with his mouth.

1 Have a tug toy in one hand and some treats in your pocket. To start the game, say "Take it!" and offer your dog one end of the toy. Once he grabs on, the game can begin.

2 After the dog has learned to take the toy and hold on, cue him to "Drop it!" frequently.

3 As soon as your dog drops the toy, reward him with a treat and praise. Eventually, the reward for dropping the toy will be starting the game again.

"We call it the check-in game," says Ann. "Dogs love it."

To play, hide somewhere when the dog isn't watching, and make it the dog's job to seek you out. When the dog finds you, give him a reward. This teaches the dog to keep an eye on you because you might disappear, and also that the dog will be rewarded upon finding you. This game builds support for a much desired behavior: having your dog want to come to you. Ann's dogs like to know where she is, so they'll search for her.

Puppy Parties: Indoor puppy parties provide enrichment by exposing a puppy during her socialization period to a variety of situations while the novelty is fun instead of scary. Invite friends to visit, and let everyone touch the puppy so she can learn she has no reason to be afraid of new friends. Ask your friends to wear something unusual—like a funny hat or a colorful pair of sunglasses—to get your puppy used to the different appearances people can have. The puppy will grow accustomed to being handled and jostled, as well as to being around lots of people.

"Since we started our puppy socialization classes here, our return rate for puppies has dropped dramatically because the classes are teaching the puppies how to adapt to real-life situations," Ann says. "Our volunteers help us socialize the puppies by participating in the daily classes."

The Best Friends puppy socialization classes start with basic handling: touching the pup's paws, ears, tails, and so on, mimicking the kind of handling the dog likely would get at a veterinarian's office. Then the puppies learn some basic training, such as performing a "Sit" and "Down," walking on a leash, and coming when called. Finally, they interact with other puppies, get exposed to their crates, and meet plenty of people. Everyone who meets the pup acts happy and excited, which builds the dog's confidence and decreases the likelihood of fearful behaviors when she meets people and dogs in their new homes. Fearful, unsocialized dogs are more likely to bite or to seek isolation as solutions to their anxiety.

Socialization should continue throughout the dog's life. Taking the dog to a dog park or to the home of a dog-owning neighbor will allow her to practice and maintain some of the good behavior skills she began learning at a young age.

Learning New Tricks: Teaching a dog new skills, like shaking "hands" or doggy dancing, is another way to keep his mind engaged. A broad range of tricks can be taught by using shaping and targeting techniques. Trainers use a technique called shaping to encourage behaviors a dog probably would never do in the wild, such as shaking a paw. Such skills develop when the trainer reinforces one small action that points toward the ultimate goal, and then builds upon it incrementally until the larger trick is learned.

A practical example would be to teach a reluctant dog to enter a crate; you could reward him any time he took a step in the right direction. Over time, the dog will move closer and closer to the crate until he feels comfortable to go inside. Or, on the fun side, you could teach a dog to spin by rewarding him every time he did something resembling turning in a circle. As he repeats the step to earn treats, variability in his movements causes the dog to perform some actions more like a spin than others. Those movements are reinforced, and so on, until the dog reaches the final goal. Scientists call this repeated process of taking small steps "shaping by successive approximation."

Targeting is a simple behavior that can be used for shaping more complicated ones. Targeting is a behavior in which the dog uses his nose or paw to touch a target, such as your hand or an object. As soon as the dog touches the target, say a marker word or click.

Then follow immediately with a treat, which tells him he's done something right. One behavior Ann has taught using targeting is to have the dog push a VHS tape into the player with his nose. She also used targeting to teach Bubba, a Best Friends dog, to grab a tissue from a box whenever she gave the cue by faking a sneeze.

As an example of using targeting for shaping a more challenging behavior, Ann has used peel-off sticky notes, whose bright colors make them stand out from their surroundings, as targets. A sticky note as a target may be placed next to a light switch on a wall, and the behavior of turning on and off a light switch can then be shaped.

Old Dogs, New Tricks

It's a lie. You *can* teach your old dog new tricks. In fact, you ought to do just that, for the sake of your dog's mental health. Most dogs want to play and learn, from puppyhood through the end of their lives. Mental enrichment, such as being introduced to new toys and games, helps them make the most of their sunset years.

Science has demonstrated that mentally stimulating puzzles, lessons, and social activities may help senior citizens ward off the onset of Alzheimer's disease. Veterinarians believe the same is likely to be true with dogs: Enrichment slows cognitive decline.

A panel of animal behavior specialists meeting at the 2002 American Veterinary Medical Association Convention in Nashville reported heartening results from laboratory enrichment tests. Old dogs exposed to enrichment activities including new tricks and tasks were better able to learn than those who lacked such enrichment. Enriched environments apparently kept dogs mentally sharp, well into old age.

Targeting can be used to introduce a fearful animal to potentially scary objects and new people. Targeting could help a horse to put aside her fear and enter a trailer, for example. Best Friends trainer John Garcia used targeting to persuade Rush, a dog rescued from Beirut, to go near a brush in return for a reward. Slowly, Rush grew accustomed to the unfamiliar object, associated it with good things, and then began to enjoy the times when John would groom his coat.

There are many other tricks that you can teach your dog. Many are standards, such as playing dead or picking up toys. Others can be ones that you make up. The book *The Only Dog Tricks Book You'll Ever Need,* by Gerilyn Bielakiewicz, advocates positive reinforcement for teaching tricks. The book includes tips on how to get a dog to ring a bell to go outside, give high fives, and open and close the refrigerator door.

Teaching a dog to fetch a newspaper, overcome a fear, or stand on her hind legs does more than demonstrate a dog's skills. It cements the dog's bond with her human companion, makes her feel more confident, and even expedites future learning. The more tricks a dog knows, the more quickly she is able to learn new ones. So, training a dog to do tricks teaches her how to learn.

Many resources are available for teaching dog tricks. They include books, videos, and professional trick classes. Jen finds trick classes to be fun for people as well as their dogs. Everyone relaxes and has a good time, she says.

Outdoor Fun

Outdoor activities provide maximum physical exercise. Dogs free to run and play copy many of the actions of their ancestors in the wild: running, hunting, digging, following scent trails, and interacting with other dogs and humans. There are plenty of outdoor activities to keep a dog busy beyond the standard walking and fetching a ball or stick. When combined with mentally stimulating play, they offer enrichment.

Start by looking around your own yard. If you have the space, consider adding a sandbox or a designated area for digging.

"My favorite thing is to give a dog a sandbox. My dogs love to dig. I can never move to a place that has a lawn, because they are in love with this sandbox I call my yard," Jen says, referring to the sandy, dry soil of southern Utah.

Try burying toys in the sand and letting your dog dig them out. Locating them by scent stimulates the mind, and uncovering them burns energy. When your dog brings up a familiar toy, she'll probably be very happy.

Dog Parks: Berkeley, California, opened what has been recognized as the world's first dog park in 1979. Ohlone Dog Park began as an experimental project under the supervision of the Ohlone Dog Park Association. Today, the association's idea not only has become permanent in Berkeley, but has also spread to several hundred dog parks sanctioned by local governments throughout the United States. Dog parks offer a large fenced area for dogs to play with other dogs while off leash. They typically have double-gated entrances and exits so dogs cannot bolt through the opening, benches for people, shade trees, a water supply, trash cans, and tools or bags to pick up and dispose of waste. Many also have some of the elements of the sport of agility, described later in this chapter. People know their pets can run free in dog parks without worrying about them getting loose.

Dog parks aren't for everyone. Don't take puppies without vaccinations, females in heat, and dogs who bully other dogs. Don't take your dog if she's aggressive toward other dogs, has been poorly socialized, or has yet to learn to come on cue. Without such basic control, people may find their dogs misbehaving.

Jen says she finds that dogs sometimes get into trouble when their people stand around. People should keep their dogs busy by walking around the park and keeping their dogs moving, she says. Dogs enjoy following scent trails at the park, discovering new objects, and running with other dogs. After a half hour at a dog park, your dog should feel much more relaxed. However, dogs and their human companions might do best by staying a shorter or longer time, depending on circumstances. People should stay alert and keep watch over their dogs to keep them safe and out of trouble. They should know when their dogs don't want to play any more, and take them home.

On the Trail: Dogs can be excellent running and hiking partners. When trained to follow you closely off leash or run or walk at the end of a loose lead, they match your speed and enjoy your company. Unlike some human running partners, they don't make you feel guilty if you go too slow or stop too soon. And they don't brag about their own running experiences.

Wait until your dog is an appropriate age, as determined by your veterinarian, before you start running with him. Running before a dog's bones mature, particularly when doing so on hard pavement, may cause physical injuries. When you do decide to start, begin slowly. Your dog needs to break into the sport the same way you did, a little bit at a time. Some dogs may need to build stamina, although healthy dogs of many breeds can run for hours. A bigger issue is the toughness of your dog's feet. His footpads need time to grow tough; otherwise they may bleed from contact with raw concrete. Stay on soft dirt paths if you can, as they are the best surface for both of you.

Remember that your dog needs water just as much as you do. Teach your dog to drink from a water bottle or carry a collapsible doggie dish that you can fill at a fountain.

Be absolutely certain you can control your dog if you try to run with him off leash. The last thing you want is to see your dog bolt into traffic or tangle with another dog. Parks with dirt trails are a good place to run with a well-trained dog off leash. Remember to learn the local leash laws in your neighborhood to know where it's permissable to have your dog off leash.

Getting Wet: Many dogs love water. They can cool off and enjoy splashing and playing. Elderly and heavy dogs get an added benefit from swimming: Buoyancy takes some of the weight off their legs and reduces the stress of exercise.

You don't have to live near the ocean to expose your dog to water sports. Even in the arid Utah canyons that surround Best Friends, creeks trickle through the brush, inviting dogs to cool off on a hot day. Lakes and ponds near your home may have recreation areas that allow dogs. Community pools sometimes offer a day in the summer when dogs are welcome to exercise in the water. And even if you don't have access to such opportunities, you can always put a hard, plastic kiddie pool in your backyard and fill it with a garden hose. Don't get the inflatable kind, as a dog's toenails will puncture it. Your dog may prefer the water to be cold, or warmed a bit by the sun.

Running, walking, and playing fetch translate well into water sports. A dog who chases a ball on land may get even more stimulation and enjoyment from plunging into the ocean surf or eddies of a shallow creek during a game of fetch.

Tennis Balls and Flying Discs: A simple game of catch is a tried-and-true way for many parents to have fun with their kids. A simple game of fetch with your dog can also be a reliable way to enjoy outdoor time with your pet. Some dogs seem to have an innate talent (some might say obsession) for chasing tennis balls and bringing them back to you—just to have you throw them again.

Other dogs may need to be taught this game. A good start is to get your dog excited about picking up and dropping the ball: Begin by putting the ball on the ground in front of her and praising her when she picks it up. Next, ask her to drop the ball and reward her when she does. Repeat this step a few times and work up to having your dog hold onto the ball for a few seconds before dropping it. Next, try throwing the ball a short distance away. Praise your dog when she chases it and picks it up. Then give her the cue "Fetch" as she returns to you with the ball. When she reaches you, ask her to "Drop it" and give her treats when she does. Once she's mastered the trick at a short distance, start throwing the ball farther away to add more fun to the game.

Catching a flying disc, like a Frisbee, will make your dog think more than she would when chasing and catching a ball. The ball follows a predictable path shaped by gravity. The flying disc follows a different set of physics equations, borne of the envelope of air that supports it and the spin that imparts its lateral movement. A dog who catches a flying disc must not only run after it, but also watch, analyze, and adjust her jump to its descent.

Play can be as simple as tossing a disc in your backyard or competing in the Frisbee Dog World Championship. Border collies and whippets seem to take to the sport naturally, but many breeds aren't quick to catch on. For them, Jen recommends you begin training by rolling the disc along the ground and encouraging your dog to grab it. Or you can start by tossing the dog a soft toy for a while and then substituting a soft, plush flying disc. End by having the dog bring you the toy or disc and drop it at your feet. Reward

Learn to Fetch

1 Start the game by dropping the ball on the ground right in front of you. As soon as your dog picks it up, praise her.

Good dog!

... Drop it!

2 Next, ask her to "Drop it" and treat her when she does. Repeat the picking up/dropping it behavior several times, working up to having your dog hold the ball for a few seconds before you cue, "Drop it."

3 Next throw the ball a short distance. Praise when she picks it up, then cue her to "Fetch." When she reaches you, cue her to "Drop it" and reward when she does. When she is reliably fetching, toss the ball farther.

with a treat. It may take some time before a dog can graduate to jumping and catching a hard plastic disc, and some dogs may never get there.

Practice on a soft, grassy area free of broken glass, bricks, holes in the ground, and other hazards. Warm up with short throws. As you move on to longer tosses, your dog will get a real workout, so be sure to have water on hand.

Flyball: Got a dog with energy to burn? Flyball may be the sport for her. It's got a fast pace and crazy, hyperactive feel. Many people and their dogs love it, and it's a terrific way for dogs to use their brains and burn energy. As with any canine sport, you'll want to see if Flyball is one that both you *and* your dog can enjoy.

The sport arrived in the 1970s, when inventor Herbert Wagner of California created a tennis ball launcher that a dog could activate with the touch of a paw. Dog training clubs in Toronto and Detroit began incorporating the ball launcher into some simple games, which evolved into the first Flyball tournament in 1983. The sport now is regulated by the North American Flyball Association.

According to the association's official rules, Flyball pits two four-dog teams against each other, one at a time, in a relay along a 51-foot race course. Each dog runs the length of the course, clears two sets of regulation jumps, and triggers the Flyball box at the end. The box fires a ball into the air. The dog catches or retrieves the ball and carries it back along the course to the starting line. The next dog in line then sets off along the same course and performs the same skills. The first team to have all four dogs finish, error-free, wins. The association has more than 700 clubs with more than 16,000 registered dogs.

Flyball participants loudly express their enthusiasm for the game, barking nonstop as if encouraging each other. High-energy dogs such as border collies and Jack Russell terriers are popular among competitors.

"It's good for the dogs who were bred to work all day," Ann says. "They need that outlet. That's what they live for."

Agility

"Agility" isn't just a quality of a physically active dog. It's also the name of a rapidly growing sport where dogs learn to navigate a series of obstacles. An agility course can be run competitively, pitting highly trained dogs and their trainers against one another, racing against a clock. Or it can be adapted just for fun by setting up a simple course in the backyard, at the dog park, or virtually at any piece of ground and run for mental and physical stimulation. At all levels, the bottom line is having fun.

The activity began almost as an afterthought in the late 1970s. Organizers at a dog show in England wanted to find a way to keep the crowd's attention between events. Some of the show's officers wondered whether dogs could be trained to navigate obstacle courses and jump, twist, and run in a way similar to horses at show events. A year later, after training their dogs, they put on a demonstration of speed, agility, and obedience that sparked a movement. Within a short time, trainers on both sides of the Atlantic Ocean were devising agility courses of ever greater creativity and complexity, encouraging their dogs to amazing demonstrations of physical and mental achievement.

An agility course has five basic components that can be arranged, repeated, and modified in nearly infinite ways:

Jumps. They come in tests of height, length, and precision. Dogs must clear bars set up like track hurdles and go through suspended tires. Agility courses typically have more jumps than any other component.

Contact obstacles. These consist of light-colored contact zones that dogs must touch or receive a penalty. Touching the zone slows the dog and increases the chances of safely navigating the obstacles. Three common contact obstacles are the A-frame, the teeter, and the dogwalk. An A-frame consist of two flat panels that form an inverted V shape, with their bottom edges on the ground and their tops joined to form an ascending and descending slope. The height of the V's apex averages about six feet. Dogs must touch the contact zones at the bottom of the panels as they ascend and descend. The teeter, as its name suggests, is a simple seesaw that the dog walks across, shifting the plank's weight from one side to the other; the dog must touch the contact zones coming and going. The dogwalk is a narrow, elevated walkway, again with contact zones at the on- and off-ramps.

Tunnels. Dogs must go through large, flexible tunnels that look like giant clothes-dryer exhaust tubes and emerge at the far end. Some tunnels are open at both ends. Others require the dog to push through a flap to continue on the agility course.

Weave poles. Like Olympic skiers negotiating gates as they go downhill, dogs must weave left and right around a series of upright poles. Missing a gate results in a penalty.

Table. Just when a dog starts to get up a good head of steam, he has to demonstrate he is under control. The dog must leap onto a low table and then go into a sit or down position and hold it for five seconds. If the dog releases too soon, he gets a penalty.

The sport highlights a dog's athleticism, but it's really a team effort. The dog's human companion must provide detailed training to get him ready to compete. The trainer begins at home or at a park by teaching the dog to master each skill of agility. Then, the trainer must teach the dog to go from obstacle to obstacle in response to a series of verbal and/or hand cues. Finally, on the course itself, the trainer must run with the dog to guide him from obstacle to obstacle. The object is to negotiate all of the obstacles, error-free, in the shortest amount of time. If the dog doesn't complete all of the obstacles, completes them in the wrong order, knocks a bar off a jump, or otherwise makes penalty-worthy mistakes, the judges may disqualify the dog from the competition.

The sport has attracted a following because handlers and dogs both find it addicting. Agility dogs love to run, play, and have fun with their human companions. As they begin to master the complexities of agility, they respond with joy to the stimulating environment. They sense the excitement and want to do well, making the use of positive reinforcement with rewards of toys and treats, a particularly appropriate training method. People often find that through doing agility with their dogs, they form stronger, more emotionally satisfying bonds.

Many organizations sponsor formal agility competitions. Check for local clubs in your area that may organize them; details about competitions can typically be found via a Web search. Dog owners can try training on their own with a book such as *The Beginner's Guide to Dog Agility*, by Laurie Leach, or sign up for one-on-one or group lessons.

However, it doesn't take formal training and a competition schedule to enjoy the benefits of agility with your dogs. Nor do you have to buy expensive training equipment.

Jen encourages dog owners to create a makeshift agility course out of household items. A pipe directing rainwater from

Agility A-Frame

1 Setup: Lower the apex of the
A-frame to no higher than
four feet. Test the A-frame
yourself to make sure it is
sturdy. Have another person
with you, positioned on the
opposite side of the A-frame
to act as a spotter.

2 Approach: With your dog
on leash, approach the
A-frame and guide your
dog with your hand over
the center of the ramp.
If needed, use treats or
a toy to lure him across
the obstacle.

3 Up and Over: Move your
hand as needed to lead
your dog up and over
the obstacle. The spotter
should stay right beside
your dog to prevent him
from falling or jumping off.

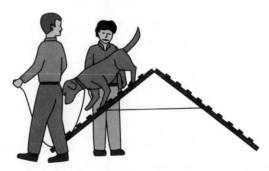

the base of a downspout becomes a low hurdle when propped on a rock. A plastic garbage container becomes a tunnel when the bottom is removed. Teeter-totters at a nearby park become mentally and physically challenging obstacles for a dog to master. Giant wooden spools—the kind used for transporting heavy cable—become instant tables for dogs to jump atop for a controlled sit.

You can even incorporate elements of agility into a daily walk, Jen says. Look for a bench for your dog to jump on and walk along, rocks to climb, and different surfaces to pose challenges. That can turn an ordinary walk into the equivalent of the trailside fitness courses for humans.

There's no special breed required for formal or informal agility. Some organizations sponsor competitions among purebreds, whereas others welcome mixed breeds. Dogs of nearly any age can do well. Senior dogs and puppies may benefit from low-stress, low-impact versions of the sport, particularly if the dogs' bones are weak or still growing. Because all dogs have their own personalities, you may not know whether your dog takes to agility until you start to work with him on the simplest of obstacles. However, some traits are definite pluses for a dog learning agility:

High energy. Agility is not for a couch potato—human or dog. Training and competition can be quite demanding.

Confidence. Dogs may have it when they start, or develop it as they go along.

Good health. This includes weight. Obviously, an overweight dog won't be as fast as a slim, healthy one. However, agility exercises promote good health.

Body types conducive to running and jumping. Low-slung, long-backed dogs, such as dachshunds and bassets, can enjoy agility, but they may have to compete at a lower impact level than other dogs. High-impact work can put stress on the spine of a short-legged, long-backed dog, potentially contributing to disc injuries.

Nose Work

It's such a natural sport, it's surprising nobody thought of it sooner. "Nose work" has only existed for a couple of years. It requires dogs to find specific scents by sniffing for them, and ends with the dog being rewarded. It doesn't take fancy equipment or a big investment, and dogs love it. Tracking scents engages a dog's brain. When she follows a scent trail, a dog processes multitudes of information that odor-challenged humans can only guess at. The mental stimulation is so intense that it can leave a dog happily exhausted.

"Five, ten minutes a day of scent tracking and they are just tired," Ann says. "They don't bark. They don't pace. They are just tired."

You can start a game of nose work by hiding a treat inside one of several nearly identical boxes. You should always use the same box for the treat or scent, until you start hiding treats outside the boxes, so the scent doesn't get spread around. Mix the boxes up as you go; don't keep the box with the treat in the same location each time, or the dog will quickly make that association. Encourage your dog to begin sniffing the boxes for the treat. Keep sessions short at first; keep the dog wanting to do more.

A formal version of the sport, called K9 Nose Work, is sanctioned by the National Association of Canine Scent Work. The sport took its inspiration from working dogs that help law enforcement agencies. K9 Nose Work trials put dogs through the challenges of finding scents in a variety of environments while working against a clock. Hiding places include outdoor areas, buildings, vehicles, and a field of boxes. Nose work does take some training. Visit the K9 Nose Work website (www.k9nosework.com) to find out more information on workshops and classes.

Lure Coursing

Dogs called "sight hounds" hunt by what they see (see Chapter 1), not what they smell. For them, a sport called lure coursing provides excitement and enrichment. They chase an artificial lure, designed to simulate a running rabbit, through a field filled with jumps, obstacles, and turns. The lure moves by remote control through a playing area that can be as small as a baseball field and as large as a half mile long.

Sight hounds typically focus on the lure with great intensity and follow it over the entire course. They usually don't need special training to follow the lure because of an innate desire to chase small animals, but other breeds may need to be encouraged at an early age to pick up the sport. Dogs running all-out stress their joints. Therefore, dogs must be one year old, beyond the bone-growing stage, to compete.

Competitors run at top speed to follow the lure. Accomplished lure-coursing dogs learn to try to anticipate which way the lure will turn and cut the edge off sharp turns. The satisfaction dogs receive from the chase prompts owners to line up for their turn at the course.

Earthdog Trials

Short-legged hunting dogs aren't built for lure coursing, but they've got a sport of their own designed for their compact bodies. Earthdog trials send breeds such as the terriers, who were bred to hunt vermin, into an underground network of tunnels. At the end of one tunnel lies the quarry, usually a rat behind a protective barrier. Earthdog competitors compete to see how quickly they can follow the scent of the quarry to the end and then "work" the quarry by barking, scratching, or otherwise actively engaging it.

Canine Freestyle

Doggie dancing, officially called canine freestyle, is a set of choreographed moves between dog and trainer, often performed to music, that the trainer has taught the dog to do on cue. Dance moves include synchronized kicks, spins, crawls, and other maneuvers such as the dog weaving between her human partner's legs. "It's another way to have fun with your dog, and to get moving and not just sit around," says Ann. "Part of it is, you take what the dog does naturally and add a few more behaviors."

For example, when Ann dances with her adopted dog Sarge, she choreographs moves to his heeling, backing up, and doing a "commando crawl" on his belly. Some moves are taught by luring the dog with a reward in the hand, such as a spin move executed by the dog's nose following a circular motion with the hand holding the treat. Ann also captures fun or interesting behaviors when she sees them and incorporates them into the dance. Mason, a foster dog, naturally turns his head and backs up when he wants attention, which Ann reinforced with rewards and got him to perform on cue. Odd behaviors, when performed on cue, become impressive dance moves.

"Training and performing freestyle should be fun for your dog," Ann says. "If your dog isn't having fun, figure out how to make it more enjoyable for her."

Freestyle dance moves include:

Heel forward and backward. The dog walks beside you, matching her gait to yours, and even backs up when you do.

Leg weave. The dog moves back and forth through the openings formed by your legs as you walk slowly forward with big steps. This move requires excellent coordination between the dog and trainer to prevent collisions and tripping.

Spin circles. The dog turns clockwise or counterclockwise in a complete circle.

Play bow. The dog's rear end remains in the air as she lowers her chest and front legs to the floor.

How to Choose

No matter what kind of personality you and your dog have, there are an endless number of ways for the two of you to have fun together. When trying to choose an activity, keep in mind what your dog likes to do as well as what you like to do. If your dog is uneasy around large groups of other dogs, then the dog park is probably not the best option. He may prefer the one-on-one nature of a hike with you. If you're nervous about competitive performances, perhaps agility competitions might not be the best activity. Remember, for exercise and enrichment to happen, you both have to enjoy it. Pick the activities that share the greatest overlap with both you and your dog's interests, habits, and personality quirks.

Top Tips

•Like humans, dogs get enormous benefits from mental and physical enrichment throughout their lives. Adding indoor and outdoor games to their lives leads to a happier relationship for both of you.

•When selecting activities for your dog, choose ones that fit her unique personality. Finding good forms of enrichment requires an understanding of what makes your dog tick.

•Choose activities that appeal to you as well so you'll be more likely to do them with your dog.

Showing your dog what is appropriate chewing material will help keep her from gnawing on your shoes and other off-limits items.

Nobody's Perfect

Sylvie came back. The bearded collie mix was adopted from Dog-town and went home with her new owner. But things didn't work out. Sylvie peed in her new house, and not just once or twice. Although some female dogs have problems with incontinence, Sylvie could hold her water for hours if she had to. She got mixed up though and had several accidents inside. Perhaps her owners mistakenly thought punishment could be used to teach house-training. She came to fear her human companions' behavior and avoided peeing in their presence.

"She learned that if she had to go to the bathroom, she had better find a spot where people could not see her," says Ann Allums, who worked with Sylvie after her return. "The punishment made her associate going to the bathroom in the presence of people with bad things."

When Ann walked Sylvie on a leash, it took at least a month before she began to feel comfortable relieving herself while Ann was there. Ann found a simple way to begin: letting Sylvie off leash so she could do her business while nobody was watching. Ann did this at first so the dog could go potty without getting stressed out. This wasn't the final solution. Ann gradually started positioning herself closer to the dog when she was going potty to help her overcome her fear. When Ann took the dog back to her house, she found Sylvie actually was well housetrained when given the option to go outside.

Urination and defecation are natural bodily functions. If you punish a dog for performing them, she gets terribly confused about your intentions. Often the dog reacts by finding a place to hide when the time comes to attend to those functions. Owners later find surprises in the bottom of closets and out-of-the-way corners of the house.

At first, the intensity of Sylvie's phobia caught Ann by surprise. She took the dog to an all-day adoption event away from the Best Friends sanctuary. For eight hours, Sylvie waited at a pet store for someone to choose her to be a forever friend. Nobody did. All the while, Sylvie refused to relieve herself, even when she was walked on a leash. She just couldn't go while people were around.

At the end of the eight-hour adoption event, Ann packed everything in her van, including Sylvie. Ann drove a bit and then left the van to check the home of a dog who had been previously adopted. In the short time she was gone, Sylvie relieved herself all over the front seat.

Rather than get upset, Ann looked at things from the dog's point of view.

"She was so afraid to go in front of us," Ann says. "That was very enlightening."

An Uncommon Approach to Common Problems

All dogs exhibit behaviors their owners would like to eliminate or modify. Not all fall under the umbrella of major problems, the kind that result in dogs being labeled incorrigible or sent to sanctuaries such as Dogtown. Some are as common and as simple as house-training issues, excessive barking and jumping, digging, chewing, and other natural behaviors that can be problematic in a home. Many are relatively easy to identify, analyze, and correct.

That was the case with Sylvie. Trainers worked with her to relearn housetraining and overcome her fear of going potty in front of a person. After she had mastered those behaviors, she found her way into a caring forever home.

Trainers at Best Friends know that the best way to change a dog's behavior is through positive reinforcement. The key to eliminating undesired behavior is to show the dog that every time they perform the preferred behavior, they are rewarded with a better outcome.

"If you get a dog to like the behaviors you like, then both of you are successful," says trainer Pat Whitacre. "You've got to trade up on behaviors. And it doesn't have to be a much bigger trade-up."

Every training session develops the relationship between dog and human. Some relationships exist on the order of drill sergeant to private, or bully to victim, with dog owner trying to coerce or browbeat a dog into compliance. Dogs typically modify their behavior in response to punishment, but they won't be as strongly motivated as they would be if the relationship with their person is one of friendship, based upon a foundation of love and trust. Rewarding a dog for right behaviors gets her to choose them for her own reasons—which happen to coincide with those of her trainer.

Pat often finds himself trying to explain things from a dog's point of view when an owner seeks help with behavioral problems. "If someone says to me, 'Why won't my dog do what I want?' I say,

'Why would he want to do that?' " Pat says. "It makes them think about why a dog would actually choose a particular behavior."

When addressing any of the behavioral problems described here, start (as always) by observing your dog. Try to find out when, how, and why he does what he does before turning to what you plan to do about it. When you encounter unexpected problems or behaviors that are a significant departure from your dog's normal behavior, begin by having your veterinarian do a thorough examination of your dog to rule out medical reasons for the behavior you are seeing. You could unnecessarily frustrate yourself or your dog while delaying necessary medical treatment by trying to train away problems that only appear to be behavioral in nature.

Once you've got a clean bill of health, you can start to work on the problem. A holistic approach is best. Some behaviors, such as excessive chewing, may result from a lack of mental and physical stimulation. Others may stem from inadequate socialization. You can try to redirect a dog's behavior in more positive ways, but the solution may require finding ways to add more activity or better relationships in the dog's life, stimulating her brain and relieving her boredom (see Chapter 6). Show your dog the right behavior and reward her for doing it, and you're halfway home.

Housetraining Mishaps

You step out of the house for just a moment to go to the mailbox at the end of the driveway. When you get back, you discover your dog chose that very slim window of time to relieve himself on your carpet.

You're probably very angry, but your best strategy is to control your emotions and not say anything or punish the dog. The damage is done. Your window of opportunity to educate the dog about housetraining has passed—at least until he has to go again. Corrections that happen after the owner finds the stain are not connected, in the dog's mind, to the act of going potty. Corrections are connected to what the dog is doing at the moment when the correction occurs. If the dog is punished when the owner gets home, he learns to expect that outcome when his owner returns home. In other words, the punishment is connected to the owner's arrival, not the behavior of house soiling, which occurred hours earlier, in this case. But there also are problems in punishing a dog caught during the act of wetting or soiling indoors—and, as already stressed, Best Friends does not modify behavior with punishments. As with Sylvie, a dog punished while relieving himself learns to hide the act to try to escape the punishment.

All you can logically do when you find a urine stain is to take the dog outside to be sure he's completely finished. Then clean the stain with an enzyme-based solution to remove the odor. Your dog will read any lingering smell as an invitation to repeat the act on that same spot sometime in the future, so make sure your cleanup is thorough.

Spending a few minutes cleaning the stain will give you time to think. Try to remember the dog's actions before the accident. Did he just eat or drink? Might he have seemed nervous about you leaving the room? Did the dog exhibit any signals—might he have been trying to tell you something? How can you prevent this from happening next time? Play detective: Some dogs bark to indicate that they need to go outside to relieve themselves. Others scratch, whine, pant, or pace. Some even stare at their owners, as if inviting the question, "Do you want to go outside?"

"People write me and say, 'He's so brazen, he just pees right in front of me,'" Ann says. "Well, that's great! Dogs don't potty indoors out of spite. He's peeing in front of you because he's comfortable with you (and hasn't been housetrained). He's giving you the perfect opportunity to housetrain him by timely interrupting and redirecting him to the appropriate place when he gives you a signal he needs to go. It's harder to train a dog who's afraid to be seen doing it." Shy and improperly housetrained dogs may sneak away when you're not paying attention, creating and then reinforcing a habit you'll later need to undo.

The owner's misconception may be the bigget barrier to resolving housetraining issues. According to Best Friends trainers, a lot of first-time dog owners don't realize a basic fact: Dogs don't automatically know they are supposed to relieve themselves outside. They have to be shown where to do it and then rewarded for doing it in the correct place.

One way Best Friends trainers recommend is using a crate to help potty-train a pup when you can't supervise him in the house. Dogs naturally like small, defensible spaces. A crate, once properly introduced, can reduce the dog's opportunities to make a mistake when you are not there to help him learn, as a dog generally does not like to foul his own space. Don't get a crate that's too big or the dog may be able to relieve himself in one end and escape to sanctuary in the other. If you want, you can get a crate your dog can grow into and seal off part of it with a wire barrier.

Be sure to introduce the dog to the crate slowly, with short periods of confinement (see the section on crate training in Chapter 4), and keep good things like toys and kibble inside so the dog enjoys being crated. Every hour, open the crate, put your dog on a leash, and rush him to the outdoors (or wherever you have your designated doggy toilet). You may want to give a single verbal cue. ("Do your business" is a common one.) You want to use a leash for these trips so you can observe that he actually does relieve himself. After giving a cue, stand in one place,

Housetraining Correction

1 Try to catch your dog in the act, or just before eliminating in the house. Make a surprising noise such as "Eh eh!" or a hand clap to distract the dog.

2 Once you have his attention, lead him outside to the appropriate place. Try to pair a cue ("Wanna go outside?") with this action.

3 After the dog goes potty in the appropriate place, immediately reward with treats and praise.

ignoring the dog, so he is not distracted by you from "doing his business." Wait up to ten minutes for the dog to relieve himself in the yard. If he doesn't do anything in that time, put him back in the crate, and try again within an hour.

At first, your dog will have no idea why you are saying anything, but after many successful trips he will start to realize that "Do your business" is connected with potty breaks. Once your dog does the right thing, give him immediate treats and praise him with enthusiasm.

You can train the dog to go in a particular part of the yard by creating a barrier to channel him in the right direction or by taking him to the correct spot on the leash and waiting until he goes. After his success, you can give him some freedom in the yard or house for a while as part of his reward. Ann recommends not playing with the dog in the yard until he relieves himself; that way, play then also becomes part of the reward.

Keep an eye on the dog while he's in the crate. If your dog came from a puppy mill, he probably was confined to a small cage and may have learned to live in his own filth. If that's the case, you'll need to remove him as soon as he gives signs of attempting to relieve himself. Common signs include sniffing, circling, pacing, and squatting. If he does relieve himself in his crate, housetrain him before you restart the crate training. Try tethering him to you with a short leash so he's always beside you as you work, play, and relax around the house. If you see him start to indicate he has to go, stop what you're doing and immediately take him outside.

If you're crate training a puppy, remember that his bladder won't be mature enough to hold up throughout the night. You already know that a puppy age two months or older can hold his urine no longer than his age in months, plus one (see Chapter 5). So, for a three-month-old puppy, you'll need to set an alarm to get up before four hours have elapsed, throughout the night, to take the puppy out of the crate and into the yard. Be aware that puppies also relieve themselves in sync with everyday routines. You probably will want to take a puppy outdoors immediately after he eats, drinks, wakes up from sleeping, and play time.

If you see your dog begin to relieve himself in an inappropriate spot, interrupt him with a noise. Say "Hey!" or clap your hands. Rather than carry your dog outside, clip a leash on his collar and let him walk out with you. If you catch him in time, he will finish his business outdoors and you can praise him.

When you take your dog outside because you think he's got to go, treat it like a business transaction. Ann recommends not paying attention to the dog until the deed is done. Wait until after the dog relieves himself before playing. Dogs—especially puppies—tend to get caught in the spirit of play and forget that they have to relieve themselves. They may do only a little bit, or none at all. Then they get put back in their crate because, the owner believes, they apparently didn't need to go. Once they relax inside, however, the problem becomes evident.

Absent a medical problem, every dog should be capable of being housetrained. If applying vigilance, using a crate, keeping to a schedule, and giving praise still don't resolve the problem of your dog urinating and defecating indoors, you still may not be supervising the dog consistently. If you just can't solve the problem, check again with your vet to rule out medical or dietary issues. Urinary tract infections, especially in female dogs, may cause them to go more frequently, about every half hour or so. Diabetes may cause a dog to drink and urinate excessively. Foods that upset the stomach or cause loose bowels, such as turkey, may also be to blame. A veterinarian could prescribe medication to tighten the sphincter muscles. However, the drug contracts all muscles, not just the ones that control the bowel and bladder, and can cause a dog to exhibit anxiety. Medication should be given only for valid medical reasons, not for routine housetraining.

If you have an adult dog who's housetrained but still needs to relieve himself every few hours throughout the night, you've got only a few choices. You could set an alarm to let him out at regular intervals or install a doggie door—a flap the dog can push through to let himself outside. Don't overlook the option of "litter box" training for small to medium-size dogs. In theory, there should be no size limit, but it might take a litter box the size of a wading pool for a really big dog. Another option might be to train the dog to eliminate on potty pads in the house.

To train a dog to go through a doggie door, begin by taping the flap so it is out of the way and the dog can see a clear pathway through the opening. With the dog inside and you outside, call the dog. You may need to stick your head or hand through while calling. Once the dog passes through the door, praise and reward him. Practice this a few times, and then reverse the direction, having the dog enter the house from the outside. The next step is to repeat the process with the flap down. You may need to show your dog that the flap moves when pushed. Reward and praise each time the dog goes through the door. Then combine the dog's newly formed door habits with rewards and praise when he relieves himself outdoors.

Excessive Barking

What is excessive barking? Whatever you determine it to be.

Some people can't stand to hear a dog bark twice. Others don't mind when their dog barks, particularly if she is calling attention to something or someone, such as a stranger at the door. And barking that's excessive at one time, such as two o'clock in the morning, might be OK during another time, such as the middle of the afternoon.

To decrease barking, you need to socialize your dog to feel confident around all sorts of people and in many places, which will reduce the urge to bark. Provide your dog with enjoyable chew toys to occupy her mouth and keep her mentally and physically engaged. Finally, teaching your dog to bark on cue might solve the problem. To elaborate: A dog taught to bark once on cue and then to stop for a reward will associate the single bark with a good thing. If you do not reward multiple, unsolicited barks, your dog may find barking for no reward less desirable.

If you've got a problem with your dog barking, make a chart of when and where the act occurs, and, if you know, what prompted it. You'll soon see patterns developing. Your dog may bark when she sees another dog, hears something noisy in the street, or gets frustrated or bored when kept alone in the backyard. Use the patterns to target undesirable encounters and actions that may be setting your dog off. Your dog barks to communicate; try to figure out what she is trying to say.

Some dogs use barking as a means to gain attention. At Dogtown, a dog named Cabby barked so much that trainer Tamara Dormer wondered if she was deaf. Whenever anyone came within Cabby's range of vision, she barked nonstop until the person left. The staff figured they would have to work on the barking if Cabby was to ever be adopted. They hung a sign on the door to her run that said, "If I am barking, don't approach my gate." When a trainer approached the pen, Cabby barked and the trainer turned away. That denied Cabby the attention she had been trying to solicit with her barking.

Eventually, the trainers slipped her rewards in the moments when she was silent. Cabby learned she would get attention only when she was quiet, which made her want to change her behavior to earn what she wanted. With repeated successes, those moments began to grow longer. Now, Tamara says, Cabby barks only about 20 percent as often as she used to.

If your dog is barking for attention, you may find it hard to keep from reprimanding her. Fight the temptation. Any attention, even when given in a scolding tone, may act as a reward that tells the dog her gambit to solicit a human response works without fail. When your dog begins to bark for your attention, ignore your dog or quietly move away from her. As soon as she's quiet for a few moments, give her attention or move closer. The dog will soon make the connection between silence and the attention she craves.

"A lot of people, when their dog is barking, speak the dog's name sharply," Tamara says. "If they do, the dog thinks they are just barking back, having a conversation." Better to capture, and reward, her quiet moments. The *pop* of a clicker, described in Chapter 5 (see "Clicker Training," page 125), can help a dog pinpoint the behavioral moment you want—in this case, silence. Use rewards to build up the dog's silences, extending new rounds of silence by a couple of seconds before giving the treat.

Ann's dogs bark to alert her to people at her door. It's an instinct for dogs to communicate information to their packs. Ann prefers to have her dogs bark a few times and then stop. She uses the words *Thank you* as a cue for her dogs to be quiet, but you could use any word, including *Settle*. Then Ann checks to see what set the dogs on alert, which demonstrates to her dogs that she took care of the situation. "They know I am aware of it," she says.

Remmi, a dog living at Dogtown, barks out of boredom. That's a common reason for dogs making excessive noise. You can't leave a dog alone all day in a yard without giving him something to stimulate his mind and body, or else he will make his own games.

The Dogtown staff treated Remmi's barking by taking him for long walks, giving him toys to play with, and finding his favorite thing—throwing him a tennis ball. If your dog barks out of boredom because he's confined to the backyard for long periods, then housetrain him and bring him inside. Not only will this muffle any barking that may annoy the neighbors, but it also will keep your dog from digging, escaping, and otherwise getting into trouble.

Dogs also bark out of excitement or fear. You can lessen those barks by managing the dog's environment. For example, while in the car, if your dog barks at things she sees outside, put the dog in a crate or in the backseat and obscure the windows with sunshades. Reward the dog for being quiet on car trips. After a few days, when the dog has shown she can be calm, remove the shades or let her ride next to the crate, and give rewards for periods of silence. If the barking returns, put the sunshades back up, or return her to the crate, and start again.

Tamara fostered a rottweiler once who got upset whenever he spied a tractor-trailer while riding in a car. Once Tamara made the connection, she started distracting the dog with treats long before passing or being passed by a tractor-trailer. The dog eventually stopped barking at the big trucks, she said. "He never liked them, he never calmed entirely down, but he would get to where he just sat there and kind of growled at the glass," she says.

Motorcycles scared her first dog. Tamara wondered whether the dog was afraid because he didn't know what to make of them. Luckily, someone parked a motorcycle on the sidewalk where she walked her dog. She let the dog sniff it, bumper to bumper, for 15 minutes. After that, he never barked at motorcycles again.

Barking can be contagious, with one bark triggering the next dog in line in a neighborhood, and then the next, like a canine version of "doing the wave" at a sports stadium. Beware of trying to teach a dog to be silent by introducing a second dog into the household. It's possible that a calm dog may work to quiet an excitable one. It's also possible that the opposite may occur, with the barking dog teaching the quiet one to speak up. You may end up with two barking dogs for you to retrain, instead of just one.

Remember, don't try to stifle barking entirely. Some barking is beneficial, as when a dog alerts you to potential danger (see Chapter 2 for the different kinds of barking). Consider a compromise: Allow your dog to bark only a few times instead of nonstop. To do so, interrupt the barking with a noise (such as a loud clap or a bell) to surprise your dog into silence. Reward that silence with lots of praise and a treat. Your dog has done his job of alerting you, and you have rewarded him for ending the barking after that.

Jumping on People

Jumping up can be cute when your puppy does it. But it's not so cool after the pup grows into an adult dog, or has muddy paws, or can knock you down. Get control of your dog's jumping before it gets out of hand. Ann recommends training your dog to jump only when you ask for it (on cue) and incorporating the training with commands to have the dog sit or lie down on cue, as outlined in Chapter 5.

Dogs jump up because they want to greet their human companions and receive attention. Often the behavior is accepted when the dog is young and his owner has just returned home to his happy puppy. He may even enjoy the reception from the small dog. It's good to feel close bonds with a dog, but failure to correct jumping at an early age reinforces the behavior and makes it more difficult to correct.

As with barking for attention, correct a dog who jumps by ignoring the action and rewarding him when he does what you want—putting all four feet on the ground. If you tell him to get down or to sit, you're only giving him what he wants—that is, attention. If you try to punish the dog for jumping up, you may really confuse him. The dog may respond to what he perceives to be your anger by trying to be even more friendly, jumping even more enthusiastically, and bringing on even greater punishment. If you're not careful, you can train your dog to demonstrate submissiveness in anticipation of a negative response to greeting. That's why some dogs pee on the floor when they say hello.

Ann says she also discourages jumping by bending to be closer to the dog. Excitable dogs may like to put their faces close to those of their owners. Bending closes the gap and may be effective when paired with a cue to redirect the dog to sit or to play with a toy. Be careful if your dog is overly exuberant; bending over an excited, jumping dog can result in a "face butt," which might give you a black eye, a split lip, or even a bloody nose. Remember, never put your face close to a dog you do not know as you do not know how the dog may react.

You can help your dog learn control. It's a big event for your dog when you come home after being away for a few hours, so give your dog time to calm down before giving him attention. Ignore the dog for a few moments and walk to another part of the house, giving your dog time to take the edge off his excitement. Wait until your dog sits before you pet him and give him a treat.

Next, you can reinforce this behavior with friends. Have a friend come to the door. Ask your dog to sit, and invite your friend inside. Instruct your friend to pet your dog if the dog remains in a sit. If your dog jumps up, ask your friend to go back outside for a minute. Your friend might have to exit and enter

Jumping Correction

Dogs jump up to greet us and to get our attention. So the true solution is to take away the motivation for the behavior—by not giving him any attention at all for jumping up.

1 If your dog jumps up, don't look at him, don't talk to him, don't touch him, don't tell him "Off," don't knee him; just cross your arms and turn away from him.

Good boy!

2 When your dog stands or sits calmly, reward him then with attention and praise.

multiple times to help your dog learn how to get the attention he wants without jumping up.

Once your dog has mastered these lessons at home, you can try the same tactics while you are out on a walk with him. On your walks, you may encounter strangers and you will need to advise them to ignore your dog, turn away, and say nothing if he begins to jump up. In advance of her dog encountering a stranger, Tamara often announces that her dog is in training, and she gives the same instructions as she would give the friend in the previous scenario. If the stranger is a child, an older person, or someone who looks uncomfortable with dogs, Tamara avoids passing close to them. You may have to set up your dog with some "practice strangers" to train her. After a lot of repetition, a dog will build a habit of greeting all people, friends and strangers, without jumping up on them.

Make sure you reward only for the desired behavior; dogs may have trouble figuring out what you want unless you're clear. "I had a dog in class who jumped up, and I ignored him," Tamara says. "When he put his feet on the floor, I rewarded him. He started putting the chain of behaviors together, so he jumped up, sat, and got treated." To break this undesirable behavior chain, pause several seconds after the dog jumps up and before you give him attention for standing or sitting.

While you and your dog are working on these lessons, try to set your dog up for success by going slowly and patiently through each one. If your dog is regularly jumping on people or you're in the early phases of teaching him not to jump, it's best to avoid putting him in situations—such as encountering strangers on a walk—that require a behavior he has not mastered yet. In short, do not advance to more challenging circumstances before you're confident in his mastery of the earlier ones. If he can't refrain from jumping on you as a greeting, it's better to work on that before advancing to greeting friends and then new people. When out for a walk, walk him far enough away from strangers so he cannot jump on them. It will take a lot of practice to build up good habits and make your dog a master of good manners.

Digging

Dogs dig for reasons that make sense to a dog. It's fun. It creates a cool hole to lie in on a hot day. It provides mental and physical exercise. But it may tear up your yard. If you don't want your dog to dig, you can try to control it with barriers and by directing the dog to dig in places you have designated and have made more desirable.

Ann and Tamara love watching their dogs dig. Some dogs pant with happiness as they churn through loose soil and sand. But the two trainers are not keen on dogs digging in flower beds. Their solution is to teach the dog where it's OK to dig. To do that, they mark off sections of their yards.

"Dogs don't know the difference between this part of the soil and that part. But if you give them a line, it's easier to teach them what's off-limits" Ann says. Visual barriers, such as a short fence or a row of landscaping timbers, can help your dog understand the concept of a border. Remember that you want your dog to be as happy as you are about his choice of which side of the border he chooses to dig into. By burying fun "treasures" where you want him to dig, you can help make it his favorite spot. A sandbox is ideal for designating a border and making burials quick and simple. It's easy for the dog to see where the box starts and stops, and to dig in the loose grit. If the dog heaves out too much sand, you can replace it cheaply.

To control inappropriate digging, lead your dog to the fenced or bordered part of your yard where you want to encourage him.

When he digs there, praise him. If he starts to dig somewhere else, interrupt him and call him back to the designated area. You may have to do that ten times in the first hour, but your dog should eventually make the connection. The same principle works indoors: If your dog tries to dig up the edge of a carpet or rummage through a pile of dirty clothes, redirect the behavior to an acceptable spot outdoors or to an acceptable activity in the house. Your dog could be telling you she's bored.

You may have to do some detective work to head off stubborn digging. Tamara says she noticed her dog Buck dug in her garden only after she had done the same. Buck apparently liked to churn the freshly loosened soil. Tamara realized that every time she planted a new flower bed, she would have to monitor Buck until the soil compacted and he would lose interest. Dogs also may dig if they hear rodents tunneling underground. The solution may be to remove the burrowers and thus the temptation.

There are some alternatives to redirecting destructive digging. One method is to bury chicken wire a few inches under a layer of dirt. When the dog's paws come in contact with the wire, he'll stop. Or, if your dog digs at the base of a fence, you can line it with rocks. At Best Friends, fences are deeply buried and lined with sidewalks. Dogs can't dig out, and by walking on the concrete sidewalks, they take the sharp edges off their toenails.

Some trainers advise owners to discourage digging by putting a piece of dog poop in a freshly dug hole. They say the dog won't want to work his paws into the mess that occupies the bottom of the hole. Tamara and Ann don't think the idea has much merit. A dog who finds an unpleasant surprise in a favorite hole may just decide to start a new hole elsewhere. Or, if you have a dog who likes to eat poop, like one of Ann's foster dogs, you may be inadvertently giving your dog a reward by refilling the hole every day.

Mouthing

Mouthing is different from biting. When mouthing, a dog licks or puts his mouth on your skin, without any intention of doing harm. The dog may apply soft or medium pressure, but doesn't clamp down as hard as he would when biting.

Dogs mouth each other while still puppies in the litter as a form of playing. They usually learn how much they can bite without inflicting injury or ending the play. Puppies separated from their litter at too young an age may not have had an opportunity to learn these lessons. Although many dogs outgrow mouthing, some continue to exhibit the behavior in adulthood. They may mouth their owners when they come home at the end of the workday or when they're particularly excited.

To put a stop to mouthing, provide a dog with a healthy alternative. Give him something he can mouth or chew as soon as you come home, or as he begins to mouth you. A Nylabone or other chew toy makes an excellent choice. If your dog still chooses to mouth you instead of the toy, try teaching him to be more gentle. When he begins mouthing, make a startling noise, such as "Ouch!" He may startle and stop; then praise him as soon as he takes his mouth off you. If your dog continues the mouthing behavior, walk away and ignore your dog. He will associate the lack of attention with the behavior and, hopefully, cease doing it.

Don't grab the dog's mouth and hold his jaws shut. This action scares the dog, and he may not see the association between his behavior and you physically assaulting him. Much better to try the strategies previously mentioned, which help him to be more gentle when he feels human skin and teach him that mouthing will not get him the attention he's looking for. If you physically suppress the mouthing, he won't learn how to inhibit himself around humans.

Chewing

While chewing is a normal dog behavior, it can become a nervous habit and can be a symptom of anxiety (see Chapter 8). Best Friends trainers find that dogs often use their mouths as a creative outlet not only for anxieties but also for boredom and excitement. A dog named Starsky got so worked up when going for a walk that he sometimes grabbed the pants leg of whoever held his leash. The trainers gave him a toy to carry in his mouth during walk time, and *voilà*, that solved the problem.

Other dogs try to chew their leashes while they are being walked; if the dog is a vigorous chewer, she may chew through the leash and run away. Some owners may avoid this problem by switching to a leash made of metal chain. For most dogs, the change in texture is enough to curtail the behavior, but it could also result in a bloody mouth for a dog who continues to try to chew it. Tamara found a creative solution: One day while walking a leash-chewer to the Dogtown clinic, she gave the dog her own soft leash to carry while she was being walked on another leash. "She didn't chew through it," Tamara says. "She was just happy to have it in her mouth."

Tamara applies the same rule for other destructive chewing: If a dog is chewing something you don't want her chewing, take it away and offer her something you would prefer she chew instead. Better yet, deny her access to whatever she wants to chew. Dogproofing your home before you bring home your new best friend will set your dog on the proper path (see Chapter 4). Keeping a new puppy from ever having a chance to build a habit of chewing forbidden objects is the single best thing you can do to encourage appropriate chewing behavior. Be sure you're aware of where you are keeping things that your dog might be interested in: You may know your daughter's stuffed bear is not a chew toy, but your dog might not

Chewables and Unchewables

Chewable: Pig's feet. They're hard and flavorful. You can find them in most pet supply stores.

Chewable: Sterilized beef bones stuffed with liver, cheese, or peanut butter. Buy the sterilized bones in a store and stuff them yourself.

It Depends: Rawhide strips. Some dogs love them and chew them slowly. Others have digestive troubles after eating them or tear into them so quickly they choke. The best advice is to never leave your dog unsupervised when he has a rawhide chew, unless it is the granulated type.

Unchewable: Corn cobs. They can lodge in the intestines and prove difficult to remove. They don't show up on X-rays, so the blockage may be hard to diagnose. Folklore once held that chewing corn cobs cleaned a dog's teeth. Although that may be true, they're not worth the risk.

Unchewable: Chocolate. It's poisonous to dogs. If you suspect your dog has eaten any, contact your vet immediately.

Unchewable: Glass. Some dogs like to chew discarded lightbulbs or accidentally ingest broken glass with gravel. If your dog has eaten glass, feed him lots of bread. It may surround the glass in the intestinal tract and let it pass harmlessly. Call the poison hotline for information about physical signs of distress, and be ready to take your dog to the vet.

make that distinction. When in doubt, remove the object from the dog's space to reduce the likelihood of any accidents.

For younger dogs, destructive chewing may be part of teething, which happens at about five months of age. Dogs, like humans, put a lot of things in their mouths when they're young. Many grow out of the behavior as they get their adult teeth. Some puppies love shredding facial tissues; they may pull them from the box or retrieve them from a wastebasket. They may also pull the fluffy stuffing out of plump pillows. Offer a soft chew toy as an alternative.

Although you can buy toys specifically designed for teething dogs, you also can make your own. Try cutting a one-foot piece of ordinary rope, dipping it in water, and freezing it overnight. The cold, hard surface, which grows more pliable as it thaws, appeals to teething puppies. Or stuff a Kong toy with moistened dog food and let it freeze. Some Dogtown trainers do this often. They find it provides the same kind of cold, hard stimulation as a frozen rope with the added advantage of smelling like food. As it thaws, the dog will have to work to extract the food from the interior, providing mental and physical stimulation. (See "Food Toys" in Chapter 4.)

Some adult dogs still like to chew. To them, there is no such thing as an inappropriate object to chew on, and often the most appealing items to the dogs aren't the ones humans would want them to choose. They may include shoes, pocketbooks, and table legs. Observe your dog's chewing habits and offer a similar but acceptable substitute. For example, if your dog likes to chew the wooden rungs of dining room tables, offer her something hard, such as Nylabones or sticks from outdoors (if you don't mind cleaning up after the dog is done with them). If your dog prefers to chew soft items such as pillows or fabric, try a softer toy like a rope or squeaky chew toy.

You also can try offering the dog a variety of toys, both soft and hard to let your dog pick out the toy she wants to chew. The toys don't have to be store-bought. A lot of dogs like to play with the cardboard tubes left over from rolls of toilet paper and paper towels. Tamara saves the tubes from toilet paper and drops them in a basket in her bathroom. When her dog wants to chew one, the dog picks it out from the basket.

Best Friends trainers have differing opinions about using so-called "aversive" sprays to prevent dogs from chewing on a particular item. These products come in spray bottles and have a scent or taste, such as bitter apple, intended to smell or taste unpleasant to dogs to discourage chewing. Although a spray may work on some dogs, others may find the taste appealing. The spray also may damage what it's applied to.

If you teach your dog what items are acceptable and unacceptable to chew, one item at a time, your dog may be able to discriminate among your possessions—like your socks—and chew only a certain one and leave the others alone. If you have a dog who chews on your socks (after you have left them out), he is probably just chewing on whatever he finds, possibly because it smells like his human companions, rather than not being able to tell the difference between his sock and yours.

Partnership

Remember, the behaviors in this chapter fall under the umbrella of normal doggy behaviors. Dogs bark. Dogs chew. Dogs dig, and dogs go to the bathroom. How, where, and when they do all these thing depends on you. It's your responsibility to provide them with acceptable outlets for these behaviors to help them learn to do them in acceptable ways. Helping a dog to successfully navigate the rules and expectations of humans is important to keeping harmony in your household and an important part of your relationship.

•When addressing a problem, begin by observing your dog. Track her behavior to see when, how, and why the behavior is triggered.

•Control your emotions if angry and upset; punishment may make a problem worse, not better.

•Go slowly and patiently when teaching your dog appropriate behavior. Make sure you're both confident in his new skills before proceeding to more advanced challenges.

•The key to eliminating undesired behaviors is to encourage a dog to have a greater desire to perform the preferred behavior. Make the reward more attractive than the inappropriate activity.

•Fun can keep unacceptable behaviors at bay. Keep plenty of dog toys on hand to stimulate your dog's mind and relieve boredom.

Dogtown co-manager John Garcia worked closely with Little Girl, a Catahoula mix, to overcome her fears and anxieties.

When There's
a Problem

John Garcia noticed a newcomer wearing a red collar in one of the Dogtown octagons under his care. A red collar, he knew, meant only staff members such as himself and not any of Dogtown's volunteers should approach the dog. The color serves as a warning that the dog has special issues—typically related to aggression—and should be treated with caution. John looked at the red-collared dog and noted she wasn't showing any obvious negative reaction to his approaching the dog run's fence and gate.

"She wasn't growling, showing her teeth or displaying any other warnings, and she wasn't actively hitting the gate as she might in barrier aggression, so I figured, 'Hey the dog doesn't seem upset with my approach,' and therefore I tried to walk in," John says. "I opened the gate, and the first thing I put inside the run was my left hand." Big mistake. The dog bit John's hand and tried to drag him down to the ground.

The painful wound he received that day serves to remind him about what he should have done instead, as well as the importance of communication between dog and human when dealing with behavioral issues. He knows he should have stopped, looked at the descriptive card on the dog's cage, and closely examined what behavior the dog was exhibiting.

John got medical attention for his torn and bruised hand and returned a few days later with another staff member to try meeting the red-collared dog again. This time the introduction went well. In the time between the two visits, John thought about what might have triggered the aggressive reaction.

"At first, in my head, I did nothing wrong," John says. "The dog just bit me for no reason whatsoever. But then I started thinking about it. And I realized I did quite a few things wrong. First, I didn't try to make friends with the dog. I just immediately tried to walk into the dog's space. I didn't register the fact that the dog was brand new, was of course scared, and that I was a total stranger to her.

"If I had looked more closely at the dog, I would have seen that her whole body was very stiff and she was wagging her tail," John says. "A wagging tail does not necessary mean a dog is happy. This tail was straight up, moving side to side at a gradual pace, which tells me the dog was highly aroused in some way. She was stiff, like a metronome, not a full body 'glad to see you' wiggle."

The dog had exhibited classic signs of arousal. And dogs acting under heightened arousal tend to make what humans see as bad decisions: They run away, snap, or bite. To dogs, however, those actions make perfect sense. Most dogs, like most humans, seek to avoid confrontations, but they may be willing to do whatever it takes to restore their sense of safety.

If interacting with humans scares a dog, she may try to remove herself to a safe place to escape from the perceived threat. For example, she may try to hide in a corner or get far away. But if a persistent human pursues her, she'll realize that trying to get away didn't get her what she wanted. When this happens, the dog has only four choices: to try to flee again; to shut down or give up and surrender to the threat; to use aggressive warnings (barking, growling, snapping, charging, and so on); or to mount an actual attack to drive the threat away. The dog might go in any of the directions. She might choose not to give any warning at all and move directly into the attack. Or the dog could combine the actions in any order, such as biting and then fleeing. Any dog has the potential for unexpected behavior, and Dogtown staff members try to stay mindful of every dog's potential to use aggressive behaviors.

Identifying the Problem

It can be difficult to know what to do if your dog begins exhibiting some more serious behavioral problems. Overlooking nervousness or the early signs of aggression may lead to bigger problems down the road, so it is important to carefully observe your dog to see what may be triggering his behavior. For instance, dogs may exhibit serious behavioral issues when guarding resources, which can be *anything* they consider to be of value, including food, toys, territory, and people. Other problematic situations include interacting with other dogs or humans, or feeling isolated, uncomfortable, overstimulated, depressed, or frightened. All of these things can cause stress in a dog, and stress can move them closer to their threshold for using desperate behaviors.

In situations that could trigger potentially dangerous dog behavior, trainers proceed with extreme care. Dogs under stress require a caring human's time and patience to overcome their problems. Although owners can take the initial steps by gathering as much information as they can about the problems, they should follow up by consulting a professional for help before attempting to correct any extreme behavior. Having a professional observe your dog in person is the best option, rather than relying on email or the phone. John says he's very reluctant to give advice over the phone or email when people contact him to explain their problems with aggressive or violent dogs. He wants to see a dog's behavior in person before trying to craft a response; he fears that giving the wrong advice to callers might make matters worse, or even get someone hurt.

Similarly, a good dog training manual can help owners recognize and understand undesirable canine behavior, but extreme cases should only be addressed with the help of a professional trainer. To find one, John advocates seeking recommendations, whether via postings to Web pages or through your friends who own dogs, and checking with your veterinarian, local shelters/rescue centers, and even local groomers, who deal with a lot of dogs. Don't assume that the costliest trainers are the best, John says—he's been surprised that some of the best trainers he knows have been the cheapest. "It's not necessarily so, that if you pay an absurd amount of money, the trainer is going to be gold," he says. What matters most are the owner's comfort level with the trainer's methods and the trainer's success rate with the specific problem that is being addressed.

Diagnosing a problem yourself may be difficult, as a dog's behavior can change over time. For instance, consider the adoption of a dog who did well on a cat-aggression test. At the adoption center, he remained calm and friendly when introduced to a cat or two. Yet, when taken into a new home and shown the owner's two cats, one of the cats immediately ran away. The dog saw the cat fleeing and joyfully gave chase. That may not mean the dog was or is aggressive toward cats. Rather, it may only have been the expression of instinctive canine behavior honed over millions of years of evolution: When a dog sees an animal run away, he gives chase as hunters do with their prey.

For another example, in the following scenario, you leave for work on Monday morning after having adopted a dog during the preceding weekend. You know the dog has been housetrained and that he hasn't shown any behavioral issues to cause you concern. Nevertheless, when you return home in the evening, your house is a mess. The couch cushions have been torn to shreds, the linoleum on the floor has been pulled back in long strips like lasagna noodles, and there's urine and feces everywhere. Surprise!

This could be a result of "separation anxiety" or "separation activity." The dog clearly had a strong reaction (nervousness for the former, boredom for the latter behavior) to being alone all day for the first time in a new environment.

Dogs adopted into their forever homes after spending months or years in a shelter or bouncing from home to home sometimes display physical reactions, such as pacing or whining, as expressions of their nervous energy when they are adjusting to a new environment. But more complex behavior problems can crop up unexpectedly; these include shyness and fear, resource guarding, barrier aggression, aggression toward dogs, and aggression toward people. For all treatments, Best Friends trainers urge the continuation of positive reinforcement techniques to strengthen good behaviors in conjunction with excluding the opportunity to practice undesirable behaviors. You must show the dog what the right behavior is by rewarding it when it happens. In addition, you must prevent the undesired behavior from being practiced, or prevent it from being successful from the dog's point of view. Positive training techniques can create a solution that both parties are happy with, which produces the strongest foundation for good habits, especially when trying to overcome more serious issues.

Shyness and Fear

All living beings periodically experience anxiety. This state of uneasiness or apprehension could stem from virtually anything—from physical contact to the lack of physical contact, from uncertainty about events to certainty, and so on. For some dogs (and humans too), shyness can be one persistent source of anxiety.

Shyness in dogs manifests in many ways, from cowering and urinating, to avoidance, warnings, and aggressive behavior. Shyness can have many components. There may be a genetic predisposition that colors how a dog experiences the world, traumatic events that shape the animal's perception of the world, lack of proper socialization, or combination of all three. Some dogs are shy, and some are outgoing. Some shrink from confrontation, and some react defensively. Some may have a history of bad relationships with others, and some do not. A dog may exhibit shyness with other dogs, as well as toward people or to one and not the other. The exact origins of shyness can be difficult to pinpoint.

If your dog is shy around other dogs, you will undoubtedly see some awkwardness in her greetings with other dogs. She may not let herself be sniffed and may decline the normal rituals of friendly greeting. Often, a dog who has not been socialized properly may fear the things that they have not been adequately exposed to, such as other dogs, people, or experiences. It is possible that the dog may have a learned negative association with something or someone. Gradually exposing the shy dog to a variety of your friends, their dogs, or new things, one at a time in a safe, controlled environment, may help build her confidence and trust around others.

John urges paying close attention to a shy dog's behavior to get clues about possible solutions. He uses a Best Friends dog named Little Girl as an instructive example. When John met Little Girl, the beautiful Catahoula mix ducked every time John raised a hand

Shy Dog Interaction
A shy dog may show fear when she meets other dogs. Observe her body language to see if she is uncomfortable with the situation. Some things to look for include:

As a dog approaches, a shy dog may stiffen her body, crouch down, and tuck her tail underneath her body.

To avoid an encounter, a shy dog may turn her body away from the approaching dog and decline the greeting.

or made what he called a "big movement." He said he didn't know why she reacted that way. It's possible she had never been socialized to be around someone who spoke or dressed or moved the way he did. It's also possible that Little Girl had been socialized, but that these "big" motions had been part of being mistreated Without a complete history of the dog, he could only guess—and he's loath to do so.

"I have seen so many cases where someone says, 'This dog doesn't like men, and must have been beaten by a man,'" John says. "I don't like to pigeonhole a dog and say, 'This is why the dog acts the way she does,' because then we are ignoring her personality and probably the true reason for her actions."

It is a fact that men are different than women in many ways that dogs, and not necessarily people, pay attention to. Men have larger bodies, different postures, deeper voices, and other characteristics that people may take for granted but that dogs may find threatening. If a dog is in fact shy or fearful of men, the treatment is to gradually get the dog to associate men with good things. For example, John has men take over all of the caregiving responsibilities for the dog. Men provide water, food, toys, exercise, and all of the necessities of life, until the dog begins to link men with rewards and alters behavior accordingly.

John urges dog owners to observe their pets closely to see when and what they react to with shyness or fear to identify correlations. Shy or anxious behavior may occur at feeding time, before bed, before a walk in the evening, or only when you are present. Look for patterns and then reward the dog for calm behavior in those situations before the dog's old behavior takes hold.

Keep in mind that shy dogs very often don't respond to any of the traditional rewards for behavior. They may not take a treat, they may find the sound of your voice frightening, and they may not

Fear of Thunder *Boom! Crack!* There goes the dog.

When a thunderstorm breaks, a lot of dogs exhibit behavior ranging from mild anxiety to outright panic. You may not want to over-respond in the mildest cases. The dog may be only a bit scared, and you may choose to see if demonstrating confidence will be enough to encourage the dog to become more relaxed. Your thunder-phobic dog may be taking behavioral cues from those around her. It's possible that, if everyone stays calm, your dog will learn to tolerate an electrical storm. Similarly, if you have a second dog who's calm during thunderstorms, your mildly upset dog may take his cues from the serene dog's behavior.

Extreme cases require intervention. Thunder-phobic dogs have been known to nervously pace, jump out of windows, chew or lick their skin raw, and even self-mutilate. John Garcia suggests desensitizing a dog slowly to the sound of thunder using a recording of a thunderstorm. You can make one yourself, or purchase one off the Web, using "thunder" and "recording" as key words in a search engine.

"I started playing tapes of thunder, so low that I couldn't hear it," John says of one of his treatments. Day by day, he gradually boosted the sound. "In a month and a half, it was so loud that people flinched when they heard it. But the dogs were desensitized to it."

He recommends rewarding a dog for exhibiting calm behavior during the recordings. If a dog flinches from a burst of thunder that's a bit too loud, don't react until the dog returns to a calm state. Then give her a treat. If it is too loud, turn it down until it's at an appropriate level.

like being touched. In these situations, it is important to remember that a reward is something that the *dog* values. Very often, the thing a shy dog wants most is to be left alone. Working with such a dog includes not increasing the dog's anxieties by trying to force rewards that are not wanted.

In Little Girl's case, it seemed that her shyness was caused by lack of proper socialization. She came to Best Friends when she was around a year old, and may not have been introduced to enough people and different situations to get her beyond her fear of anything new. When John took her home, Little Girl felt overwhelmed by everything in his home that she hadn't seen before. To help the dog, John was careful not to feed into those anxieties.

"She wouldn't go by the washing machine," John says. "That went on for a couple of days until she got over that fear. Then she wouldn't go by the dryer, right next to it. She had patterns of being afraid of everything in the house, item by item, until she got used to them and could walk around her new home and have little to no fear."

Little Girl still had behavioral swings at night, when she shifted from her happy, loving moods to what John called her "streaky" phase. At night, when the lights were off, he would walk out of his bedroom and see a streak of gray flash across the floor. He would flip on the light and see another streak. He said it became clear that the nighttime streaker, Little Girl, felt edgy when she couldn't see her surroundings.

"I ignored it," John says. "That behavior started to dissipate very quickly because I did not play into it. I did not say to her, 'What's going on?' I did not say, 'You're making me anxious.' When she went streaking, I said, 'Whatever.' I did not feed into her fears, so she began to understand they were not a big deal."

When phobias persist, you can try getting a dog used to the source of her fear by desensitizing the dog to the scary thing at low levels of exposure. To desensitize a dog, you slowly introduce her to whatever upsets her so she may become familiar with the offending object or person and grow to accept it. But be judicious; don't expose the dog to what scares her suddenly and at full strength, such as loud thunder or linoleum floors. Start with barely audible recordings of thunder or by placing scraps of carpet over the unfamiliar surface, and then work your way up slowly.

John suggests trying to discover the dog's "reaction zone," which is her radius of reactive behavior, and then work to shrink it. If your dog begins to show signs of fear or avoidance when she gets within 20 feet of something or someone, then move her backward until she seems able to relax and give her a reward. As you reward the dog for nonreactive behavior, she begins to associate good things with her ability to use calm behavior. With time, patience, and a pocketful of dog treats, you can slowly decrease the distance between your dog and the object of her fear until they can be very close to each other. Remember to give the reward to the dog immediately upon her displaying the behavior you desire. Clickers may be useful tools in exercises like this. They can help to pinpoint and mark the behavior being rewarded. Be careful that any auditory marker you use is not one that frightens the dog.

Separation Anxiety and Separation Activity

Some of the most challenging problems to deal with are those that only occur when you are not at home with your dog. Not only can coping with being alone be difficult for the dog but you are, by definition, not available to intervene or instruct. These problems are commonly labeled "separation anxiety," but they may also be the result of "separation activity." Separation anxiety most accurately relates to problem behaviors related to a dog's intense discomfort with your absence. This may result in the destruction of property (often but not always focused around doors, windows, or other possible means of exit from an enclosure), injury to the dog as a result of these efforts, or self-mutilation from excessive licking or chewing on body parts. At first glance, separation activity may seem similar, but the mess you discover upon arriving home is the result of the dog finding ways to entertain himself while you were out. In simple terms, one is the product of stress and worry, the other of boredom. Neither should be confused with brief "I want to go too!" pleading that ends shortly after you are out of sight.

Although it takes a certain sense of humor to appreciate it, separation activity is the less serious of the two. The dog is not in the kind of mental distress that a dog with separation anxiety is. He is dealing with being alone by making "creative" use of all the wonderful toys—the couch cushions, piles of dirty laundry, shoes, TV remotes—that his thoughtful humans left for him. In the case of separation activity, we are the only ones who have a problem; after all, that was our stuff he chewed up! Best Friends trainer Pat Whitacre compares this situation to leaving a young child alone in the house, only to return to find that he has colored on the walls, put the TV remote in the toilet, and covered the new carpet with a nice coat of spaghetti sauce. Bored kids do kid stuff to entertain themselves. Bored dogs do dog stuff. Separation anxiety, on the other hand, involves both a serious problem for the dog and for us, because his efforts to relieve his stress create many of the same problems for us (our stuff!) as separation activity.

Because both of these problems are heavily situational, they may be difficult to spot before bringing an adopted dog home. For instance, at Best Friends, many dogs are seldom left alone for long stretches of time. They typically have plenty of people or other dogs to keep them company. But when Dogtown dogs are adopted, they may have to adapt to a world quite unlike the one they were used to. Your home may lack a constant stream of other dogs and people to entertain your new pet. She may find herself overwhelmed, scared, frustrated, or bored in her new, more subdued environment.

If your dog begins to exhibit signs of separation anxiety (or the traits of any other extreme behaviors), particularly if they are a departure from normal activity, take her to your veterinarian for a complete checkup. Ruling out possible medical issues is always an important first step before deciding on a behavioral treatment plan. Many underlying medical conditions can present as, or contribute to, behavior problems. Your veterinarian can also advise you about the possible role of medications in the treatment of separation anxiety. (Best Friends does not endorse the routine use of prescription medication to treat anxiety but understands that this is a decision between you and your veterinarian.)

As with many problems that arise in a household that more than one species shares, the solutions to separation anxiety and separation activity frequently involve multiple approaches to address all aspects of the situation. The good news is that many of the same interventions are helpful for either problem.

There is the practical matter of protecting the house and your belongings. This often involves restricting the dog's access to anything that could be damaged while you are out of the house. Crating or limiting the dog to a relatively dog-safe room may be options. In either case, it is important to first create a positive association with the area that is to be the dog's safe spot.

Crates are neither good nor bad in themselves (see Chapter 4, pages 106-108, for more on crates). At best, a crate can be a favorite cozy den that can afford a sense of security. At worst, a crate can be a cold unfamiliar jail that adds to the dog's distress. The proper crate should keep the dog safe. Although metal may seem stronger than plastic, many of the handy folding metal wire crates are not as safe for a dog with severe separation anxiety as a plastic "airline"-type crate. Many distraught dogs have injured themselves bending and breaking out of the wire-type crates.

Crates can be misused when the length of time spent in them is excessive. It is important to not let the time in a crate be dictated by your schedule alone. If you have to be gone all day and cannot go home over lunch, arrange for a friend, neighbor, or a pet sitter to stop by to help. Four hours is a long time to spend in a crate without a potty break. Another option is to not leave the dog at home. Take him with you if possible, or consider doggie day care. Either can give a bored dog more to do or an insecure dog companionship.

It is important to provide your dog with appropriate entertainment outlets when he is home alone. Enriching the environment with safe toys, chewies, comfortable beds, and sounds (music, radio, TV) can go a long way to making time alone enjoyable for the dog. Pat Whitacre often asks people to tell him what they expect their dog to do for the first 15 minutes he is alone, what he will then do for the second 15 minutes, and so on. It becomes obvious that chewing on the one toy they left him for 15 minutes will leave the bulk of the day with nothing new to do. Often we hope that the dog will just sleep most of the day, but for that to happen, we need to see that the dog gets plenty of exercise when we are home with him. This is not only a necessary outlet for his healthy energy but also being a little tired may help him appreciate those longer stretches of time as opportunities to rest.

One way to help relieve your dog's stress is to disassociate the signals that tell him you're leaving for an extended period of time. Think about what you do when you're getting ready to leave—you grab your car keys, put on your coat, pick up your bag, and go out the door. The dog sees these actions as cues that he's going to be alone for a while, which can trigger his anxiety. Practicing pretend departures—ones where you go and very soon come back—can help. First, pick up your car keys, put on your coat, and then take them off and don't go anywhere. Another time, do the same things, step out the front door, but then return immediately. Next time, do all this but go into the closet, or out the back door. Practice these departures dozens of times when you don't actually have to go anywhere. Vary the time you are outside before returning, keeping it brief at first and gradually building from seconds, to minutes, to hours. The dog will become desensitized to the cues that used to begin his cycle of anxiety because they are no longer predictive of extended time alone.

Another goal is to reduce a dog's stress by teaching him how to be OK at home alone. One useful step is to make good things happen only when you leave the room or house. This can mean giving his favorite long-lasting treat only when you leave and picking it up as soon as you return. Treats can be given in the crate if you are using one. You can make this tactic part of your practice departures, giving your dog the treat as you exit and then taking it back when you "return." The dog will realize that the sooner you return, the less time he has with his prize. A dog's regular meal given in a slow dispensing food puzzle toy can work as well. Not only can you end up with a dog that doesn't mind when you leave, but one that hopes you will leave, and stay gone a while, all because he looks forward to the rewarding and stimulating activity that will only happen if you're not there.

You can go further to reduce the significance of your exits and returns. Avoid making a fuss about leaving. A prolonged emotional goodbye may convince your dog that you too are unsure if you will ever see him again. When you return, with the possible exception of picking up the goodies you left, do not interact with your dog for ten minutes. Let him out of the crate or say hello to him after he is calm. He will see that your arrival does not change his situation for the better, but that his calm behavior does.

Resource Guarding

Food, shelter, water, human companionship . . . all are essential to a dog's life. In nature, survival depends on access to and keeping possession of valuable resources.

Dogs with resource-guarding behavior may employ the same signals as any other form of canine communication. A variety of signals may be sent to other dogs. A dog might guard by picking up a bone and moving a few feet away, staring at another dog, showing teeth, growling, snapping, biting, or chasing another dog away. Or guarding behavior could be very subtle, such as not making eye contact or passively moving something so as not to call attention to it.

Resource aggression is relatively common among dogs. It is not limited to dogs who were deprived of food during war and famine, but it becomes essential under those conditions. Dogs living in a natural state are hardwired to guard anything of value.

It's not limited to dogs who were deprived earlier in their lives but is certainly understandable for dogs who were—such as Edward who came to Best Friends from a puppy mill. After spending his life confined to a small cage without toys or bedding, when introduced to toys at Dogtown he didn't want anybody else to have them. Edward liked playing with other dogs very much, but toys were so valuable to him that he didn't like to share. He would growl to warn them away from the toys.

The same can be true for virtually any resource. A dog may guard food or a piece of clothing. He may even guard the person who takes care of him. John cites the guarding behavior of a dog named Cinder toward her owner, Kersten Muthreich. "Cinder is a great

Resource Guarding

Dogs can see almost anything—a person, a toy, food—as resources and may use different behaviors to protect them. Guarding behaviors can be very subtle (such as avoiding eye contact) or very explicit (such as growling or snapping).

Guarding can be as simple as a passive movement. Here the dog guards his bone by physically moving it away from an approaching person.

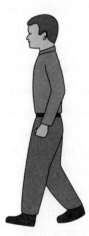

This dog is overtly guarding his person. He growls to warn an approaching person to stay away from his resource.

grrrr

dog," John says, "but if you make a move toward Kersten, Cinder will immediately come over to you and start pestering you to leave Kersten alone. If the dog preceives your actions as aggressive, she defends the owner because the owner is important and valued."

John says Best Friends employees sometimes hear of guarding behavior developing in newly adopted dogs. Some have lived in shelters all their lives, or fended for themselves in the open air, and when they finally get a home of their own, they feel they have to do whatever it takes to survive there. "In their minds, it may mean scaring everybody away. They don't want anybody competing for their resources," John says.

John has a simple formula for dogs who have food issues. If they guard their food, and their food comes in a bowl, he removes the bowl. He then hand-feeds the dog until the dog associates John with the resource of food. This is one skill where John particularly recommends getting the help of a trained professional, as not all dogs will take food gently from the hand.

John helped Heidi, a dog rescued from Hurricane Katrina, overcome her food-guarding habit. "The first thing I did was remove the association of the food with the bowl," John says. "Some of the time, it's the object, not the food, that's important. Dogs look at it as a magic bowl, because that's where they get all the food."

John approached Heidi with handfuls of food hidden behind his back. He reasoned that if he controlled the resource, the dog would learn by practice that an approaching hand might give food, not take it away. He fed the dog from his hand, six to eight times each day. That way, he says, Heidi learned she would get food all the time and would not have to protect it. As part of the hand-feeding exercise, he required Heidi to exhibit good behavior before she received her food rewards.

John also has seen guarding behavior with toys, particularly when several dogs compete over scarce playthings. If he has two or more dogs in a pen and one exhibits protective behavior over a ball, he removes the ball. He doesn't want guarding to become a habit; the more a dog practices guarding behavior toward a ball or any other resource, the more likely the dog is to repeat the behavior in the future.

Sometimes the dog tries to protect its resources not from another dog, but from his owner. You may try to take a ball away from your pet only to have him snap at you. The strategy for halting such destructive behavior is to ask the dog to make a trade. Make giving up the item—the goal of the trade—a successful exchange from the dog's point of view. "The first thing I am going to do is to trade with him, and give him something way better," John says. "That way, the dog learns that something much better comes along when I ask him to give me something. . . . [H]e learns this because it is the truth. By the way, only the dog gets to decide what is 'better.' I will use treats as much as I need to, but at the same time, I am not a 'treat trainer.' I want the dog to rely on our relationship and my praise whenever possible."

The replacement reward could be a hot dog, a dollop of "squeeze (aerosol) cheese," a pig's ear, or whatever has a relatively higher value to the dog. Dry kibble may only require a dog biscuit for the trade. A pig's ear may require a piece of chicken. Once the dog makes the connection that very good things happen, from the dog's perspective, he practically spits out something in his mouth when his trainer asks him to drop it.

John recommends repeating and reinforcing the substitution with the help of friends. The dog then begins to generalize that it's good to let go of his guarded resources no matter who asks for them, because he gets what he wants and the humans get what they want.

It's a win-win situation. The trade comes about because it's a mutually agreed-upon bargain, not a transaction enforced through authority.

If a major conflict over food or any other resource persists, call a professional and ask for an in-home visit. Bringing somebody to your home with a fresh perspective and an understanding of dog behavior can bring a new level of expertise to the problem. A professional, certified dog trainer will provide an unbiased view of the interactions between you and your dog, as well as insight into what might produce his undesirable behavior and how to resolve the problem to your satisfaction and to your dog's.

Barrier Aggression

Barrier aggression can occur when a dog feels frustrated or trapped through restraint of movement, either from access to something, or an inability to move away from something. It could occur while the dog is walked on a leash, or it could happen when a dog is confined inside a fence. Either situation may cause the dog to bark and act aggressively toward anyone who approaches her. Regardless of the situation, fear, frustration, and uncertainty probably lie at the heart of the dog's behavior. The dog feels upset because the restraint prevents her from doing what she wants or needs to do, which includes interacting with the world beyond her reach. If the restraints were not present, she might not act aggressively at all under the same circumstances.

One way to deal with barrier aggression is to reduce the number of things she is uncomfortable with. Try introducing your dog to a wide variety of people, animals, places, and things, and you may lessen the anxiety she feels. The more practiced and comfortable she becomes with meeting new things, the less reactive she will become when she encounters them.

Environmental factors may play a role in the aggression of penned animals. John notes that when he approaches Dogtown in the morning, a cloud of dust, visible from far away, hangs in the air over the pens. It's churned into existence by hundreds of paws treading the earth in their enclosures. Some dogs, like some people, prefer a low-key environment and may become anxious or frustrated when overstimulated, which may lead to barrier aggression. It's hard to know if a particular dog would show the same aggression if not confined. Some would have less frustration without the barrier and therefore less reason to react negatively. Others might still be aggressive and violent.

Best Friends dog trainers help to reduce aggression of penned dogs by having the dog learn to associate the perimeter of the fence and people who approach it with good things. They begin by tossing or handing the dog a treat every time they pass by. Soon the dog starts to hesitate before barking in anticipation of the person and the treat. This allows the trainer to give treats in response to the desired calm behavior. If the dog resumes barking during the interaction, the treats are stopped, and the trainer goes on his way. Over time, through positive reinforcement, the dog learns that her

Barrier Aggression

If a dog has issues with barrier aggression, typically he will engage in aggressive behaviors—loud barking, growling, snarling, charging, or lunging—when a person approaches or walks by his enclosure.

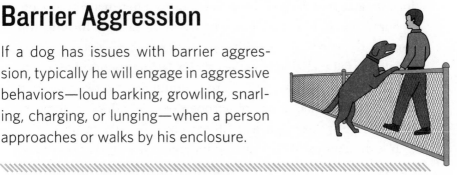

behavior affects the delivery of rewards, and she builds a new habit of calm behavior at the fence.

John uses a variation of this technique to help dogs generalize the positive experiences of people visiting their pens to others. After John has established a positive relationship with a dog, he takes a friend with him on visits. If the dog reacts negatively to the friend, John walks away and leaves the newcomer standing outside the fence—not the outcome the dog intended. When the dog quiets down, John returns; he doesn't have to give the dog a treat because his presence is a reward in its own right. After seeing this pattern a number of times, the dog makes the connection that her aggressive behavior is what makes John leave and her polite behavior brings him back and keeps him close. Dogs will always value the behavior that produces the best outcome. In a sense, the new people get to use John as a reward for calm behavior instead of treats.

Aggression Toward Dogs

Normally, when two well-socialized dogs approach each other, they go through a get-to-know-you ritual. They walk toward each other in curving lines, sniffing each others' faces and rear ends. One dog may attempt to initiate some fun with a play bow, which the other dog may accept or decline. They play, hang out together, or move on.

Some uncomfortable signs when two dogs meet include stiff posture, flattened ears, tucked tails, and wrinkled muzzles. These signals can tell each dog how the other is feeling about this encounter. All of these are ways for one to communicate to the other that he is uncomfortable. If the other dog does not notice, ignores, or takes offense at these signals, a "disagreement" could ensue.

It is difficult to avoid a rush to judgment if your dog is displaying aggressive behaviors around other dogs. No one wants to put his dog or other dogs at risk of injury by intervening too late to prevent a fight. However, one function of using these aggressive-looking signals is to convey a warning that a dog is uncomfortable with what is happening. Effectively sent and recognized, these behaviors can serve to make a fight unnecessary and to avoid further conflict. This is the reason trainers at Best Friends say "Thank you" to a dog who growls at them, for giving them a welcome opportunity to avoid more serious reactions. All of the skills that dogs require as adults are usually learned and practiced in play. From communication skills to bite inhibition and from hunting skills to mating behaviors, all are explored and mastered through nonserious rehearsal during play. Dogs interacting at a dog park may be safely establishing the rules of their relationships when they

Aggression Between Dogs
When two dogs meet, sometimes the encounter can take a negative turn. Signs of two dogs not getting along include stiffened posture, bristling fur, flattened ears, tucked tails, and wrinkled muzzles. Aggressive dogs may lunge at each other and strain against a leash.

appear to fight, or they may just be dogs who enjoy rougher, noisier play. When humans intervene, especially with loud noises and agitated movements, dogs may possibly become alarmed or confused and think the encounter is more serious than it really is, and escalate their actions.

"My rule of thumb is, the louder and nastier it sounds, the less likely it is to be serious," John says of encounters between dogs. "If it's a quiet fight, oh yeah, it's far more likely to be serious. They want the fight to continue."

John understands that dogs growl as a way to communicate. When two dogs growl at each other, they communicate; often, the information they share leads to a peaceful resolution. Growls potentially help them avoid a fight. But some dogs aren't skilled at this communication or may be unduly aggressive toward other dogs. Dog aggression is a dangerous issue, and one that owners need to address with caution for their own safety as well as their dog's. Try to reduce the likelihood of your dog becoming dog aggressive by socializing your young dog, introducing her to as many other dogs as possible, and continuing to practice throughout her life.

If dog aggression is a concern, a basket muzzle may help to reduce the risk of injury. John has trained dogs to enjoy wearing a muzzle by associating it with food. Over a period of three days, he trained the dog to eat food placed inside the muzzle, as if it were a small and flexible food bowl. Getting the muzzle strapped onto the dog's face requires desensitization, and it comes in small steps. After using the muzzle like a bowl, begin poking bits of kibble through the front of the muzzle so the dog has to keep his face in the empty muzzle to get his treats. The next step is to clip on the muzzle and give two or three treats, and then unclip and remove the muzzle and stop giving treats. The dog will come to associate getting treats with wearing the muzzle. Once the dog looks forward to wearing the muzzle as a means to get treats, you can pair the muzzle with a leash and take the dog for a walk, so the dog gets treats and the added pleasure of a fun outing.

Muzzling doesn't eliminate the problem, however; it only minimizes the risk from it. At the first sign of a dog beginning to react negatively to the approach of another dog, try giving a familiar cue for a sit or down, and then reward the dog if he is able to focus and respond to your request. If requesting a familiar behavior focuses the dog's attention away from the other dog and brings a reward, you are at the correct distance to begin counterconditioning and rewarding calm behavior. If the dog is unable to focus on your cue, you are too close and need to begin from a greater distance. Practice this with a friend who also has a dog on a leash, and over the course of an afternoon, you may put a dent in your dog's aggression toward your friend's dog. It may take repeated contact with other friends and other dogs before your dog begins to generalize the good behavior around other dogs. Remember that if your dog cannot respond to you or refuses to take a treat, he's telling you he's too aroused by the situation to pay attention to food. That's valuable information; you need to lower your dog's arousal level for effective training to occur.

As always, consult a professional to help you in any cases of dog-to-dog aggression. It is dangerous and irresponsible to allow your dog to react violently around other dogs. A dog might get hurt—or worse.

People Aggression

What does people aggression look like in a dog? It depends on the dog. You might see a dog who appears to be ignoring you and assume it's not displaying fear or aggression. But look closer. Is the dog freezing, or purposefully moving himself away from you? The dog may be trying to communicate his sense of unease, and you may find yourself getting bit if you're not alert to the signs and act accordingly.

"Every time I have been bitten, it was my fault," John says. "I have either ignored something or knowingly put myself in danger."

The goal is to try to understand a dog as an individual, and to be observant of the signs the dog is displaying and the many potential behaviors they could indicate. Some dogs may fear nearly everyone or those with some similar quality, or they may pick out individuals. Many dogs can dislike a particular person without extending their negative reactions to others; very few dogs like everyone all the time.

As we mentioned earlier, start your analysis by ruling out medical complications and any painful injuries. Dogs who snap or bite may be only trying to minimize their discomfort by avoiding painful contact with humans or other dogs. Make sure your dog has a clean bill of health before moving on toward situational factors that may trigger the aggressive behavior.

If you have a dog who demonstrates aggression toward people, your first responsibility is to keep everyone safe and ensure that no one gets bit. This can be as simple as moving the dog to a secured space in the house or the backyard when other people are in the house and not taking the dog out in public without a muzzle. You should only expose your dog to people in a controlled environment.

Understand that dog-human communication is a two-way street. While you are reading a dog's body language, the dog also is reading yours. If you approach another person or dog with a fearful body posture, the dog may recognize that something is amiss.

An instructive example of human-dog communication occurred when John took Georgia, a pit bull rescued from Michael Vick's dogfighting ring, into a swanky Beverly Hills hotel. At that point,

Georgia wasn't inclined to be aggressive, but she was fragile enough that human behavior could make her nervous. Georgia responded well when treated calmly and normally. Georgia can appear intimidating, with her cropped ears, broad chest, and well-muscled frame, and that appearance could put off people who didn't know her. When John took her into the hotel lobby the first time, she wore her regular old green collar attached to a leash. People backed away, consciously or subconsciously, from what they saw as a powerful, intimidating dog. Their actions made Georgia nervous.

So John and Georgia walked out together. John changed Georgia's look: He gave her a hot pink collar and leash and hot pink tank

Behavioral Trade-Offs
As you try to modify your dog's behavior, you may find that progess on one issue can result in new behaviors that will also need to be addressed. Bingo, who came to Best Friends from a shelter, lived in a protective emotional shell. One day when John Garcia visited Bingo in his run, the dog bounded to him and began jumping and pawing. "I was thinking, 'This is awesome,'" John says. "But at the same time, he was exhibiting undesirable behavior because he was clobbering me."

Every time you help a dog become more confident, you will automatically begin to see more normal dog behaviors. A dog who has shut down may cause you no trouble, but this is not the same as being well trained or socialized. When a dog gains the confidence to begin acting like a healthy, normal dog, you will have the opportunity and responsibility to teach her the skills she needs in a world she shares with humans.

top that said, "Biscuits are a girl's best friend." When they walked back inside, people came and cooed over her. Their relaxed, friendly approach put Georgia at ease, and everyone enjoyed the encounter. So if a dog is making you nervous, there is a good chance that your mood is not putting him at ease either and is possibly making the encounter worse. It's best not to push an encounter until you feel more comfortable.

Similarly, John doesn't rush working with an aggressive dog. If he feels apprehensive about the encounter, he waits until he feels more confident so he can demonstrate relaxed, controlled body posture. He advises that you can never let aggressive behavior go unchecked. Dogs repeat behaviors that work for them. If growling and snapping at a scary visitor made the visitor go away, the dog is likely to repeat the behavior next time. Soon, the aggressive behavior becomes a habit. It's easier to prevent bad habits from taking root than to correct them once they are established.

If you've got a dog who's aggressive toward anyone, you've got a problem that may lead to serious consequences if not corrected. Get a medical checkup, and then seek expert advice.

Take Action

If your dog begins displaying any behaviors that concern you, be proactive about what might become a serious problem. Take action by having a full veterinary assessment of your dog to rule out any underlying medical causes for changes in your dog's behavior. Discuss your observations with your vet, who may be able to recommend a course of action. If you determine the problem is behavioral, you could consult a trainer to work with you on using simple training techniques to help your dog. Anytime you are working on behavior modification, use caution and patience. If you determine that the problem requires more specialized help, your veterinarian can recommend other professionals; these include a behavior counselor, a certified applied animal behaviorist, or a board-certified veterinary behaviorist.

•In cases of potentially dangerous dog behavior, proceed with extreme caution and care to protect you, your dog, and others from harm.

•Take action quickly if you think your dog is developing behavioral issues. If the problem is ignored, it can develop into something more serious and potentially harmful.

•If your dog begins displaying behavioral patterns associated with serious issues, get a medical checkup to rule out any underlying medical cause.

•If you are concerned about behavioral problems, consult a professional. Your vet can help you find the help that you and your dog need.

•Dogs under stress require a caring human's time and patience to overcome their problems.

Nochi's kiss to trainer Ann Allums shows how building a trusting, lifelong relationship with your dog rewards everyone with joy and love.

Epilogue

Ten Takeaways for a Fulfilling Relationship

Having a positive relationship with your dog takes more than good intentions. Like human relationships, bonds with a dog grow strong through the application of patience, love, and dedication. Your best friend deserves nothing less. Although there may seem to be a lot to learn, especially for someone who's not had a lot of experience with dogs, the dog experts at Best Friends emphasize the following ten keys to success.

❶ Commit to a lifelong, loving relationship with your dog.

Perhaps you've noticed something subtle in the preceding chapters. Every time the book called for a pronoun to be used in place of the word *dog*, or to replace a dog's name, the word *she* or *he* appeared. That was no accident. Your dog is not an "it." She has feelings and emotions just like you. Her love is genuine. Look upon your dog as a family member, giving her the same time and affection as you would a person dear to you, and you will be rewarded with the most loyal, attentive, loving friend you could imagine.

Tamara Dormer recalls being dumbfounded by a neighbor's question when she got ready to move to Utah from North Carolina. "Are you going to take your dogs with you?" the neighbor asked. How could she not? Having dogs limited her housing choices and time away from home, but she considers living with dogs to be part of who she is. If you have a dog, find a way to continue living with her—in whatever physical, financial, or emotional state you're in.

Still, on rare occasions, a turn in family fortunes may make it impossible to keep a dog. Sometimes for good reasons—the dog doesn't tolerate a new baby, or a caregiver has grown too old or ill to continue raising a dog—a family has to make the painful decision to part ways. It happens. But such decisions should never be made lightly. Your dog has grown to depend on you and will be traumatized by the end of your relationship. If you absolutely must give up your dog, commit to finding a new home for her that is good or better than the one she shares with you.

❷ Every dog is an individual. Adopt the dog who is right for you.

Stereotypes about dogs are just as wrong as stereotypes about people. Some Labrador retrievers don't like to fetch a ball. Not all hounds howl. Some small dogs are mellow fellows, and some big dogs are doggy dynamos. Every dog is an individual.

Just as it's almost always a bad idea to propose marriage on the first date, it is riskier to adopt a dog sight unseen or within moments of meeting. Take some time to get to know a prospective adoptee. Watch the dog's behavior at the shelter or in his foster home. Go on a doggy date, if you can, or have a sleepover at your home. Consider fostering the dog yourself. Gather as much information as you can about whether the dog you're considering matches who you are today, and who you might become in the future. Come to understand a dog's personality before choosing him for adoption.

For example, you may think that because you live in an apartment and work downtown all day, a small dog might be right for you. Could be. But so could a calm, larger dog. Older dogs may exhibit a sedentary lifestyle more appropriate for someone who's gone all day and can't regularly take a dog for hikes in the woods.

Once you've brought your new dog home, recognize that she has her own individual set of likes, dislikes, quirks, and traits. For instance, you may have purchased a big cushy dog bed for her, only to find that she prefers the cooler surface of the kitchen floor. Michelle Besmehn recalls that her beagle Barnum had a favorite snoozing spot in the open, cozy bottom tier of her bookshelf. You may begin with a set of ideas about what your dog will like and dislike—but you'll need to manage those expectations as your dog grows more comfortable in your home and as different behaviors emerge. As long as behaviors are not destructive or harmful, embrace your dog's personality and appreciate the quirks that make him unique.

❸ Be positive in all things.

Any time your dog does something you like, acknowledge it. Give him a "Good boy!", a scratch in his favorite spot, or a treat—whatever your dog considers a reward. Seek out these moments when your dog is doing good things and recognize them—rather than seeking out and calling attention to things he does that you don't like. Rather than punish your dog for unacceptable behavior, ignore it. Give attention to the positive behavior to eliminate the negative. Using positive training tactics will strengthen your relationship, making it all the more enjoyable for you both.

Tamara recommends filling a cup with kibble at the start of a day and giving your dog a little reward when he deserves it. It could be when your dog is chewing a bone instead of your shoes. Or when he is being quiet instead of howling. Or when he looks at you when you call his name. Aim for at least 25 "Good boy!" moments every day. Your goal should be to empty the cup by day's end. Such rewards will not only reinforce your dog's good behavior, but also get you looking for positives instead of negatives in the life you share with your dog.

The flip side of reward-based training is preventing bad behavior from being successful. When you reward your dog for the behavior you'd like to see, you're showing him what he's supposed to do. Punishing the bad only tells the dog what not to do, but doesn't communicate to him what the appropriate choice may be. "I like to reverse the questions about dog training," Pat Whitacre says. "If someone says to me, 'Why does my dog do that?' I say, 'Why wouldn't he want to do that?' and 'What should he do instead?' It makes them think about the behavior they actually want to see and what would motivate the dog to choose that behavior over another."

❹ Your dog needs socialization and enrichment.

Socialization is an important part of a dog's life at every stage. Beginning when a dog is a puppy, teach her to react positively when meeting new people, new dogs, and new situations. If you bring a puppy home, plan to have her meet a hundred new people within her first few months. Get her comfortable with being handled all over her body, and teach her not to use her mouth inappropriately. When she's old enough, take her out on walks and to the dog park to have supervised meetings with other dogs.

Make a commitment to schedule time every day to spend with your dog. Give her opportunities—whether on walks or out in the yard—to run, explore, and sniff the world around her. Play games with your dog. Part of expressing your love is giving her the mental and physical exercise she needs.

As your dog gets older, keep taking her to new places and doing new things to expose her brain to novel sensations. Enrich your dog's life with new games, new toys, new routes for walking, and new challenges. Dogs enjoy mental and physical stimulation as much as people do. "They give so much to you," Ann Allums says. "You should give back to them."

Socialization and enrichment will help keep your dog from being frustrated or bored, which often leads to unwanted behaviors.

❺ Safeguard your dog's health through checkups, grooming, and proper diet.

Keeping your dog healthy and fit is an essential component of your lifelong relationship. Make sure you have a veterinarian that you like and trust. Take your dog for regular checkups to assess his overall health and to keep current on vaccinations and any preventative medications. Bring a list of any concerns and questions to each visit.

Take good care of your dog's coat, skin, and nails: Regular grooming will not only keep him looking neat and clean, it will also familiarize you with your dog's body so you can more quickly spot any odd lumps and bumps that may appear. Keep your dog at a healthy weight, and adjust his diet if he starts to pack on a few extra pounds. Obesity in dogs can lead to scores of health problems, and keeping your dog at a healthy weight can prevent them.

Michelle Besmehn points out that you may be helping an older dog, or one with problems in his joints, by keeping him on the lighter side of so-called ideal weight. "I have a 12-year-old dog, Citra, with only three legs, and I never let her get overweight," Michelle says, "because that could put extra pressure on her joints, making it harder for her to get around."

6 Set yourselves up for success.

You're in charge. That means you are ultimately responsible for your dog's actions. Set up an environment that encourages good behavior and discourages bad. If your dog misbehaves, chewing the shoes that you did not put away in your closet, realize your role in the problem and figure out what you could do better.

Dogproof your home much the same way you would childproof it. "Look at your home from a dog's eye level," says Sherry Woodard. "What can he reach?" If you don't want him drinking out of the toilet, tell everyone to put down the seat. If there are smokers in the house, raise ashtrays out of reach to prevent accidentally poisoning your dog with nicotine. Keep breakables and candles above tail level.

Controlling access also can prevent destructive chewing. Jen Severud recommends trying a crate if a dog begins to destroy household objects. The crate limits what the dog has access to, but it can also provide a sense of security. Says Jen, "At times, dogs can get anxious when they have too much room to keep track of. With the crate, the dog feels, 'This is all I have to keep track of, and this is my quiet time.'"

Behavioral problems almost always stem from a dog's needs not being met. Make sure your dog has adequate food, water, exercise, and mental stimulation. A bored dog is more likely to get into trouble than a content one.

Don't wait for a dog to start a bad habit. Be proactive, and teach your dog good manners and several cues. Once a behavior is successful, the dog is more likely to repeat it. Similarly, behaviors that get prevented progress toward extinction. So, get your dog a raw bone or a stick to chew instead of your shoes. Reward your dog for calmly sitting instead of jumping up on people. Show your dog appropriate choices and behaviors before she has the opportunity to start other less acceptable ones.

Ann wishes she had known more about how to raise a dog when she had Jazz, a cocker-sheltie mix. "I was just out of college," she recalls. "I got my first house and couldn't wait to get a dog. So I got my first puppy, and Jazz went through the whole thing—pooping in the house . . . chewing up the bathroom . . . chewing up the car. The more I know now, the more I realize that I could have done a lot more with Jazz." If you did not start training early enough, don't give up on your dog. Start training now. It's never too late.

❼ When in doubt, start with a medical checkup.

If you've got a dog who doesn't respond to your training or exhibits seemingly unexplainable behavior or sudden changes in behavior, see a vet to determine whether a medical issue may be the root of the problem.

"Any time a dog exhibits aggression, it's time for a medical check," says Dogtown co-manager John Garcia. "I want to know if the dog has any thyroid issues, or if the dog is in pain. Pain can influence aggression tenfold."

Health problems also can cause a dog to be disengaged from his surroundings, incontinent, unsteady, or display a host of symptoms that might be mistaken for bad behavior or disinterest. Grant, a Best Friends dog, raised concerns when his normal exuberant demeanor turned lethargic. Instead of speculating a reason to explain his odd behavior, the staff took him to the clinic for a checkup. Turns out,

Grant had an easily diagnosed illness and was back to his old self after medical attention.

⑧ Help your dog be all she can be.

Too often, dogs—like people—get labeled for life. But they can change. Persistence, dedication, and patience can help turn around many dogs.

Rescued from Michael Vick's dogfighting operation in Virginia, Meryl had a lot of things stacked against her. She's a pit bull terrier, a breed wrongly stereotyped as inherently vicious. She had been raised amid violence and its constant threat. She had been deemed incorrigible and unadoptable by the courts and ordered to spend the rest of her life at Best Friends. At a shelter where she was initially taken after her rescue, she acquired a reputation for being "human aggressive" for a few acts of fear-based behavior. For many dogs, it's a label that can end with euthanasia.

Patience and TLC have proved everybody wrong about Meryl. Caregivers and trainers worked with Meryl so she would learn to welcome and enjoy human contact. They made sure everyone who approached Meryl's pen offered her treats, so Meryl would begin to associate people with good things. The next steps involved taking Meryl for walks and getting her used to meeting others. Slowly, more and more people came to know and interact with Meryl, and she blossomed. Now, as long as someone she knows and trusts is present, Meryl greets new people with wiggly, friendly body language. Working with Ann Allums, she has become a star on the agility course, a great outlet for her energy and a wonderful workout for her body and mind.

After learning to trust people, Meryl has become a more trustworthy dog—easy to train, friendly, gentle, forgiving if startled, and happy. She still acts aggressively when she feels threatened, as when strangers invade her personal space. But now Best Friends knows that, and will always have someone on hand to manage the situation to help all her introductions be successful ones.

9 Appreciate your time with your dog. It's all too short.

His life is short compared with yours. Your puppy all too soon will become an elderly dog. So look at life the way your dog does, and enjoy the moment. You got a dog because you thought you'd have fun together. So do so!

Whitney's family already had a dog, Missy, when her family adopted Murphy, a mix of Labrador and golden retriever, from a neighbor. Whitney was perhaps four years old, and Murphy was just a puppy.

Whitney had a lifetime of fun with both Murphy and Missy. She dressed them up in human clothes. She tied them to her wagon and let them pull her around the neighborhood. She sneaked her dogs into the house and the car when her parents weren't looking. Murphy and Missy often accompanied the four Jones' kids to soccer practice. The dogs were a big part of the family.

Murphy was a special dog to Whitney. He tolerated hugs and shrieks and pokes and indignities. He listened with patience and with what appeared to be understanding when the Jones's children confided in him. He stayed happy.

Murphy was a constant through grade school, teenage years, a first job, and the first semesters of college. Sixteen years is a long life for a big dog like Murphy. But when you cherish the moments with your dog, you'll find yourself thinking you never have enough time together. Whitney was able to be with Murphy when it was time to let go. Years later, she still misses him.

⑩ Know when and how to say a final goodbye.

If you have truly committed to a lifelong relationship, losing your dog is losing your best friend.

As your dog grows older, signs of decreased quality of life will begin to emerge. These may include inhibited movement, loss of appetite, incontinence, vomiting, and excessive sleeping. Watch, too, for your dog trying to tell you what she already knows. "My dogs always tell me," Tamara says. "They give this look. I talk to them too. I give them permission to go. I say, 'Don't hang around for me. I will be OK. If you need to go, you go.'" It hurts to say goodbye. But it's even worse to hang on selfishly, prolonging your dog's pain along with her life.

Consult with your veterinarian about when to let your dog go peacefully and with dignity. Make important decisions in advance instead of waiting until you are grief-stricken. You may have to weigh difficult options, including whether expensive surgery might prolong your dog's life. Tamara says a good vet, like Best Friends Clinical Medical Director Michael Dix, won't tell you what to do, but may say, "If this were my dog. . . ." Having a close relationship with your vet will make having such talks easier. Whatever decision you make, it will be the right one if you make it out of love.

If it's time for a swift and painless end, be there for your dog just as you were there for her at the beginning of your relationship. Don't abandon your dog in a shelter to spend her last few hours alone. Take her to the vet and hold her during her last minutes. If you can't go, make sure someone she knows is there to comfort her.

It's a traumatic time. Children aren't the only ones who cry. Afterward, some people feel as if they could never face a repeat of such heartbreak.

But after grieving for what they've lost, most who have forged a partnership with a dog choose to start anew. Consider all that your dog gave you. Remember the past, but look to the future. Imagine how empty it would be without a four-legged friend sharing it with you. When you're ready, consider adopting another dog and beginning a new relationship with another special dog.

The human heart, like that of the noble dog, turns again and again toward love. And there are many, many special dogs out there who are waiting for friends to start a relationship with them—a lifelong one based on respect, trust, and love.

About the Authors

Ann Allums, Certified Professional Dog Trainer

Ann's passion as a trainer is to help people and dogs have healthy relationships by understanding each other better. With Best Friends since 2004, Ann provides training to the dogs, staff, and volunteers to help the dogs become more adoptable and enrich the dogs' lives. Classes she teaches to the staff include Practical Skills For Dogs, Agility, Reactive Dogs, Nose Work, Dog Introductions, Flexigility, and Canine Freestyle. Ann has a Bachelor of Business Administration Degree from Lamar University in Texas and worked for 10 years as a Computer Network Administrator, which helped hone her analytical skills. However, the rewards from training her own dogs to overcome behavior problems ultimately led to her career change. Ann lives with two dogs, a dog-loving cat, goldfish, and an occasional foster dog.

Michelle Besmehn, Dogtown Co-Manager

With Best Friends since 1997, Michelle Besmehn is now the co-manager of Dogtown. She oversees the daily care and medical needs of the hundreds of dogs cared for by Best Friends at any given time. Michelle also decides what new dogs will be accepted into Dogtown's care. She works closely with the Best Friends trainers and caregiving staff to determine the training needs for each dog and the right group for the dog to live in, and makes sure things run smoothly in Dogtown. Michelle currently lives with two dogs and one tuxedo cat.

Tamara Dormer, Certified Professional Dog Trainer

Tamara first came to Best Friends in 2004 and earned her dog training certification in 2007. She's responsible for training sanctuary dogs in basic manners and helping caregivers to work with behavioral challenges. She assists in finding the right runmates for the dogs who live in groups and monitors the initial introductions and any necessary follow-ups. Tamara consults with adopters both pre- and post-adoption to answer questions and address any problems that may arise once the dog is in the home. Tamara lives with five dogs and eight cats.

John Garcia, Dogtown Co-Manager
John Garcia is co-manager of Dogtown at Best Friends. John has been working with the sanctuary dogs since 1999. Since 2008, John's work with the Vicktory Dogs, the 22 pit bulls rescued from Michael Vick's dogfighting operation, has been instrumental in overturning unfair prejudices against this breed. John works often with one of the rescued dogs, a female dog named Georgia, to educate people about pit bulls. The pair have appeared on the front page of the *New York Times* and been on *The Ellen DeGeneres Show* and *Larry King Live* to show that dogs like Georgia deserve a second chance at a better life. John shares his home with his wife, two dogs, and a cat. They also take in a foster dog whenever they can.

Whitney Jones, Certified Professional Dog Trainer
Whitney Jones first began working with Best Friends in 2005 as part of its Hurricane Katrina relief efforts. After graduating from Chico State University of California, she officially joined the dog-training team in July 2007. Whitney earned her dog-training certification in 2009. At the sanctuary, Whitney specializes in helping shy dogs, teaching the caregivers to develop training plans and select enrichment activities and assessing dogs to see what skills they need help with. Whitney lives with her pack of seven dogs, nine cats, some fish, and three aquatic fire belly newts.

Jen Severud, Certified Professional Dog Trainer

Jen Severud began her work at Best Friends in September 2008. Before moving to Kanab, Utah, Jen owned and operated Canine Discovery Dog Training for five years in Minneapolis. At Dogtown, Jen works one-on-one with various dogs and also spends her time introducing new dogs to existing dog runs; assessing dogs' behavior to assist in finding them the right home; teaching clicker training classes to caregivers and volunteers; and writing training plans for individual dogs, while helping the caregivers implement those training plans. Jen happily shares her home with her two dogs.

Pat Whitacre, Certified Professional Dog Trainer

All dogs love Pat Whitacre, who has been with the sanctuary since 2007. Before beginning his career as a dog trainer, Pat earned a bachelor's degree in psychology and a master's degree in biophysics and genetics. He spent 30 years working in behavioral programs for humans in a variety of inpatient and community-based settings. A visit to Best Friends inspired him to use his training to help homeless pets become more adoptable and to improve their chances of remaining in their adoptive homes. Pat's current brood of animals includes two dogs, two cats, two horses, and a third dog being fostered from Best Friends.

Sherry Woodard, Animal Behavior Consultant

Sherry Woodard is Best Friends Animal Society's resident animal behavior consultant. A nationally certified pet dog trainer, Sherry has been with Best Friends since 1996 and is a former manager of Dogtown. As an expert in animal training, behavior, and care, she develops resources, provides consulting services, leads workshops, and speaks nationwide to promote animal welfare. Sherry has written more than 50 animal care, behavior, and training documents for

Best Friends that are used across the U.S. and by groups around the world. Sherry lives in Angel Canyon in Kanab, Utah, with her son, five dogs, two cats, one chinchilla, and one rat.

Michael S. Sweeney
Dr. Michael S. Sweeney is a professor of journalism at Ohio University. He has written several books for National Geographic and has published extensively about the history of wartime journalism. He and his wife share their home with their two forever friends: Chance, a Basenji mix, and Hailey, a Labrador retriever.

Further Resources

Publications
Dog Behavior and Communication

Donaldson, Jean. *The Culture Clash: A Revolutionary New Way to Understanding the Relationship Between Humans and Domestic Dogs.* James and Kenneth Publishers, 2005.

———. *Dogs Are From Neptune,* 2nd ed. Dogwise Publishing, 2010.

McConnell, Patricia. *The Other End of the Leash: Why We Do What We Do Around Dogs.* Ballantine Books, 2002.

Rugaas, Turid. *On Talking Terms With Dogs: Calming Signals.* Dogwise Publishing, 2006.

Puppies

Dunbar, Ian. *After You Get Your Puppy.* James and Kenneth Publishers, 2001.

———. *Before You Get Your Puppy.* James and Kenneth Publishers, 2001.

Training Techniques

Arden, Andrea. *Dog-Friendly Dog Training,* 2nd ed. Howell Book House, 2008.

Miller, Pat. *The Power of Positive Dog Training,* 2nd ed. Howell Book House, 2008.

Pryor, Karen. *Don't Shoot the Dog! The New Art of Teaching and Training.* Ringpress Books, 2002.

————. *Reaching the Animal Mind: Clicker Training and What It Teaches Us About All Animals.* Scribner, 2009.

Ryan, Terry. *Outwitting Dogs: Revolutionary Techniques for Dog Training That Work!* Globe Pequot Press, 2004.

Online Adoption Resources

American Society for the Prevention of Cruelty to Animals

The ASPCA was the first humane organization in the Western Hemisphere. Its mission, as stated by founder Henry Bergh in 1866, is "to provide effective means for the prevention of cruelty to animals throughout the United States."

www.aspca.org

Best Friends Animal Society

Best Friends Animal Society works with shelters, rescue groups, and members nationwide to bring about a time when there will be no more homeless pets. Best Friends operates the nation's largest sanctuary for homeless animals; provides adoption, spay/neuter, and educational programs; and manages the Best Friends Network, an interactive, online global community.

www.bestfriends.org

Petfinder

Petfinder is an online, searchable database of animals who need homes. It is also a directory of more than 13,000 animal shelters and adoption organizations across the United States, Canada, and Mexico. Organizations maintain their own home pages and available-pet databases.

www.petfinder.com

Index

Index

Index

Illustration Credits

Interior: 10, Sarah Ause, Best Friends Animal Society (BFAS); 40, Molly Wald, BFAS; 66, Gary Kalpak-off, BFAS; 90, 114, 150, Molly Wald, BFAS; 178, Sarah Ause, BFAS; 204, 234, Molly Wald, BFAS.

Cover, front: Troy Snow, BFAS
Cover, back: Molly Wald, BFAS

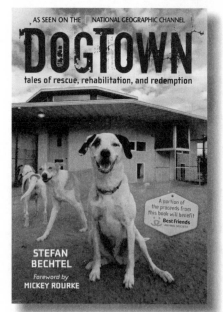
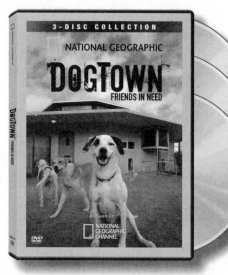
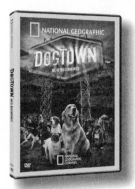
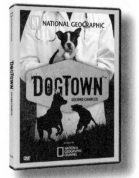